D0369359

"*Amid Passing Things* is a book as warm as it is wise. Each short chapter is a personal invitation to experience the life of faith in the middle of daily life, in the places where God comes to meet us. Fr. Jeremiah shows how to be open to these encounters in profound, simple ways."

—J. Brent Bill,
author of *Holy Silence* and *Beauty, Truth, Love, Life*

"Friar Jeremiah's *Amid Passing Things* is a touching spiritual autobiography written in short chapters like personal letters to a dear friend: honest, informal, caring, and wise. Very Franciscan."

—Robert J. Kiely,
Donald P. and Katherine B. Loker Professor of English, Emeritus at Harvard University; author of *Fair Jesus: The Gospel According to Italian Painters 1300–1650*

"As a son of Francis of Assisi, Fr. Jeremiah writes with the saint's 'spirit of prayer and devotion.' He insightfully notes how ordinary experiences give cause to pause and ponder one's relationship with God: taking a cross-country road trip, watching a woman knit in chapel, celebrating a Christmas Eve Eucharist in a parent's home, hearing about a twenty-three-year-old friend's death from cancer. *Amid Passing Things* highlights how God's grace touches us right here, right now, in the most surprising of ways. This is Franciscan spirituality at its finest!"

—Albert Haase, OFM,
author of *Becoming an Ordinary Mystic: Spirituality for the Rest of Us*

"Father Jeremiah's humble and enjoyable storytelling reminds us of the beauty and grace that is present with us as we journey through life. In an open, honest, and loving way he invites us to reflect on his stories—and the stories from our own lives—to see the goodness of God, who is with us always."

—Dr. Lisa Petronis,
Clinical Psychologist, Marriage and Family Therapist

"Everything is passing fast! How can we live towards the realities of this world so that they guide us toward the world to come instead of becoming roadblocks? Creation, friends, places, work and people can all help us toward God or block our way to him. In concise and candid personal essays Fr. Jeremiah not only allows us to learn from his experiences but models a way for each of us in our particular situations to live amid passing things with our hearts set on what lasts forever."

—Isaac Slater, OCSO,
Abbey of the Genesee, author of *Surpassing Pleasure*

"Reading this book, you cannot help coming to know something of God, while at the same time discovering how intimately he knows you."

—Sr. Virginia Joy, SV,
Archdiocese of New York Director of Respect Life

AMID

LIFE, PRAYER,

PASSING

AND RELATIONSHIP WITH GOD

THINGS

Jeremiah Myriam Shryock, CFR

San Damiano Books
PARACLETE PRESS
BREWSTER, MASSACHUSETTS

2019 First Printing

Amid Passing Things: Life, Prayer, and Relationship with God

Copyright © 2019 The Community of the Franciscan Friars of the Renewal

ISBN 978-1-64060-220-5

All quotations from scripture unless otherwise noted use The Catholic Edition of the Revised Standard Version of the Bible, copyright 1965, 1966 by the Division of Christian Education of the National Council of the Churches of Christ in the United States of America. Used by permission. All rights reserved.
Scripture texts marked (NAB) are taken from the New American Bible, revised edition © 2010, 1991, 1986, 1970 Confraternity of Christian Doctrine, Washington, D.C. and are used by permission of the copyright owner. All Rights Reserved.

The Paraclete Press name and logo (dove on cross) and the San Damiano Books logo are trademarks of Paraclete Press, Inc.

Library of Congress Cataloging-in-Publication Data

Names: Shryock, Jeremiah Myriam, 1979- author.
Title: Amid passing things : life, prayer, and relationship with God /
  Jeremiah Myriam Shryock, CFR.
Description: Brewster, MA : Paraclete Press, Inc., 2019.
Identifiers: LCCN 2019019062 | ISBN 9781640602205 (tradepaper)
Subjects: LCSH: Christian life—Catholic authors—Meditations. | Spiritual
  life—Catholic Church—Meditations. | Spirituality—Catholic
  Church—Meditations.
Classification: LCC BX2350.3 .S55 2019 | DDC 248.4/82—dc23
LC record available at https://lccn.loc.gov/2019019062

10 9 8 7 6 5 4 3 2 1

All rights reserved. No portion of this book may be reproduced, stored in an electronic retrieval system, or transmitted in any form or by any means—electronic, mechanical, photocopy, recording, or any other—except for brief quotations in printed reviews, without the prior permission of the publisher.

Published by Paraclete Press
Brewster, Massachusetts
www.paracletepress.com
Printed in the United States of America

Contents

To my father, John K. Shryock,

who while living amid passing things, always taught me,

both by word and example, to place my hope in

that which does not pass away

✻   ✻   ✻

"As we walk amid passing things,

you teach us by them to love the things of heaven

and hold fast to what endures."

PRAYER AFTER COMMUNION, FIRST SUNDAY OF ADVENT

Foreword

It was 6:30 in the morning as I boarded an Amtrak train, the Cardinal, in Penn Station, New York City. I was to arrive at Union Terminal, Cincinnati, thirteen hours later. A long time, but a short time to finish reading, reflecting, and writing a first draft of a preface to Fr. Jeremiah's *Amid Passing Things*.

I don't know this young Franciscan priest, but I had read enough of the book when I first received the manuscript to know that the voice was gentle, sincere, without agenda or self-righteous judgment. On the contrary, the voice on the page and in the silences between the words was a voice of prayer, of love of Christ and his gospel, and of love for people, seeing all of us as children of the same God of love.

Amid Passing Things is Fr. Jeremiah's story, but it is also the story of anyone who has found in God the love he or she has been looking for. God is the love who was there all along looking for us, a God revealed in Jesus Christ, who is the incarnation of the God we cannot see who dwells within us and all around us. The God revealed in *Amid Passing Things* transcends ideologies and political divisions. As Fr. Jeremiah writes simply and clearly,

> Every person is made in the image and likeness of God (Genesis 1:26). This statement, found in the very beginning of the Bible, is a reminder that the human person cannot be reduced to merely worldly categories. Too often we identify people based entirely on their political persuasions or opinions. . . .

A friend of mine recently told me that his family had to cancel Thanksgiving with his relatives this year, because of what he described as "political differences" among various family members. Both families decided that they couldn't spend the holidays with each other because of how they voted in the previous election. This story is a sad commentary on our highly charged political climate. What is tragic about it is not that people believe different things, but that they have allowed those beliefs to create divisions, even among their own family.

> Nothing is as important as our faith. But even when we disagree in religious or theological matters it is important that we continue to love the other person as God does.

These wise, guileless words come from Fr. Jeremiah's own faith, his reading of the gospel, and his Franciscan heart. We believe him when we read the words above because of where the words come from. They come from his own story, his own journey into God's love. They come from that place of silence and prayer where his own prejudices and presumptions were purified by God's Word, who is God's incarnation: Jesus Christ.

Amid Passing Things is refreshingly nonjudgmental and inclusive, as one would hope the words of a Franciscan would be. The chapters are short and readable, and the choice of subjects comes out of the author's own evolving life as a spiritual director and retreat master, two rather pretentious terms that, as Fr. Jeremiah experiences them, would more appropriately be called attentive listener and silence-and-solitude facilitator. He has a humble way, even in his written words, of welcoming, sharing, and inviting one to share, as I suspect he does in his personal listening and preaching. All the way through the reading of the text, I found myself stopping frequently and having an interior dialogue with the writer, or at times, closing my eyes and trying to see and remember the story or scene he was creating. And because it was a beautiful day as we traveled through Virginia, West Virginia, and Kentucky, I kept returning to the lovely woods, the rivers and streams outside the train window, my mind and heart open to the silence of the prayerful cell my roomette was becoming. At no point did I find myself arguing with the text or raising an eyebrow. I simply let the words lead me again and again into the love of God and all God's creatures. And amid passing things I felt the eternal. That is because Fr. Jeremiah does not condescend or make prayer and holiness something for a select few. Living the gospel is for anyone and everyone who is drawn to Christ's words and Christ's prescriptions, no matter what their calling in life is. In God's eyes we are beautiful and good because God has made us so. We have only to let God act and live through us. In so doing, we find what we long for.

As Fr. Jeremiah writes,

A few weeks ago, I was speaking with a childhood friend. . . . Unlike me, he didn't feel like his life needed an explanation. In fact, he believed there was no explanation. . . . Life was just life, nothing more. . . . After an hour or so of philosophical and theological debate together he simply asked me, "What then is the greatest thing Jesus has done in your life?" Without hesitation I said, "He has organized my heart."

In this book Fr. Jeremiah shows us how Christ organized his heart and how Christ can do that for anyone who sincerely desires him to do so, even amid the passing things of our ordinary lives, like reading a book and writing about it on a long train ride and pulling into Cincinnati's Union Terminal three hours late at 4:30 in the morning.

—Fr. Murray Bodo, OFM

Introduction

Like many people, I have often asked, "Where are you, God?" Over the years, I have found the answer to that question in varied places: in prayer, study, the sacraments, the poor, my Franciscan brothers, nature, and friendships. These are all, in some way, the more "obvious" places where anyone can find God. Still, although I feel that I've had many moments of personal, lasting discovering, providing real encounters with God's presence, I have also realized that these moments are generally few and far between.

My life as a Franciscan consists of three to four hours of prayer a day; an hour or two working on behalf of the poor, a friend, or a fellow Franciscan; and an hour or so in the evening for spiritual reading or study. If I add up all that time in these "moments of God's presence," it equals about a third of each day. What about the other two-thirds? Where is God during those times?

What's ironic about asking God, "Where are you?" is that this is the first question God asks in the Bible. Shortly after the Fall in the book of Genesis, Adam and Eve, aware of their misdeed, try to run away and hide. God asks Adam, "Where are you?" (Genesis 3:9). Just in case we think God has lost sight of Adam and Eve, or that they are simply playing a game of hide-and-seek, this question is not concerned with geographical location. God is asking our spiritual parents, "Why have you forgotten about me?"

Forgetfulness appears to be a common trait, not only for the people in the Bible, but for all of us. Before we even utter our "Where are you, God?" he has already asked us, "Where are you?"—reminding us that life is not a matter of God's being absent, but of our being absent to God.

If this is true, then it appears the great work of life needs to be learning to pay attention to God. Since our "spiritual lives" are only a small fraction of our whole lives, we must look for God in all of life and not merely reduce him to Sunday morning or times of prayer and reflection. Reducing God to merely "spiritual moments" limits God and the full life he wants to share with us.

This collection of thoughts and reflections is the result of my own desire for a deeper intimacy with God and the realization that this intimacy occurs not necessarily by becoming more spiritual, but by becoming more human, and accepting the mystery and wonder that each moment provides.

I have decided to call the book *Amid Passing Things* because it is here, in this world that "is passing away" (1 Corinthians 7:31), where God meets us. So often I have viewed the world as an obstacle to my relationship with God. *If only I weren't stuck in this traffic jam, or if only I weren't so busy, or if only I weren't placed in these circumstances,* I have thought, *then I could really be holy.* What I am beginning to discover is that the circumstances and the situations of life are not an obstacle, but actually a bridge, where God comes to meet us. This book is a mere reflection of that awakening.

1
THE MISSING PIECE

St. Augustine once wrote, "You were within me, but I was outside, and it was there that I searched for you." These words, written in the fourth century, highlight a timeless fact about the human condition: We all realize that something is missing in our life, and we believe that missing piece is somewhere "out there." The paradox, as St. Augustine discovered, is that this missing piece is within us.

When I was eighteen years old I left my family and friends. Unlike many of my peers at the time, I was not leaving for college, the military, or beginning a new job. I, along with two friends, chose a different path. Without a destination, a plan, or a specific purpose, my friends and I loaded up my Jeep Cherokee and waved goodbye to everything that was familiar to us. We were about to spend the next three months driving across the United States.

The previous twelve years of school had taught me one thing: there had to be more to life than simply going to college, getting a job, and starting a family. Was that all there was to life? I didn't know, but I was desperate to find out. The last thing I needed, or so I thought, was somebody else's interpretation of life. Therefore, college and a career had to wait. I needed to discover the truth on my own.

Even though I had grown up Catholic and went to Catholic school I never once considered that God could be the missing piece to my life. Instead, I tried to solve the questions of life with merely human resources. I dove headfirst into philosophy, poetry, and literature, believing that the answer was hiding somewhere in that vast sea of human wisdom.

As we crossed into Ohio my friends and I rolled down the windows and started screaming at the top of our lungs. We had just done something unfathomable: we left our home state of Pennsylvania. For the first time in my life I was somewhere different. The people and the landscapes were similar to what I had grown up with, but as we continued west everything began to change. Not only was the scenery changing, but it was changing me. Whether it was the Grand Canyon, the Rocky Mountains, or the Pacific Ocean, the splendor of each new place awoke in me a desire to know the Creator of such beauty.

Despite the wonder that surrounded me, the more we traveled the more confused I became. The enormous mountains and canyons that captivated me became a mirror in which I saw myself more honestly. What I saw was not the enlightened philosopher or poet I believed I was, but a child, who foolishly was placing his trust in human wisdom.

When we arrived in New Mexico I had reached a breaking point. Externally, I appeared happy and in control, but internally I was restless and lonely. Even the friends whom I was with began to annoy me. We had been traveling for two months by this time, and my hopes that driving across the country would give me clarity about the meaning of life were beginning to fade. On one level, I was a free man. I had no job, family, or other major responsibilities requiring my time or money. But on another level, I was a prisoner, because of my refusal to surrender to anything greater than myself.

As we pulled into a campsite about fifty miles north of Santa Fe, New Mexico, we quickly set up our tents and prepared dinner. Then, my friends decided to go to bed early, so I was left alone in the desert with nothing but a blanket of stars to cover me and a fire to keep me warm. I had plenty of time and space, under that great canopy in the sky, to look back over my life. "Where am I going?" I said out loud. "What am I doing with my life?" I had no answer. All I knew was that something was missing.

Suddenly the word *God* came into my mind. I was startled. It had been so long since I'd prayed or even thought about God. I didn't know what or who I meant by God, but as I continued to sit there that mysterious word began to echo inside of me. The longer I sat the more peaceful I found myself becoming. Slowly I felt the confusion inside my heart begin to dissipate. Then, out of that silence, I heard a voice from within me say, "Why are you running away from me?"

Immediately I understood.

I had placed my trust in my own mind, with the help of history's greatest thinkers, believing that I could create reality, truth, and happiness. But what I had created was my own loneliness. By ignoring the One who is Reality, Truth, and the source of all happiness, I had become a fool who deserved to be pitied rather than imitated. Before I fell asleep that night I prayed, "God, if you are real, I want to know you."

When I awoke the next morning, the world appeared strangely fresh and alive. I listened to my friends speaking from inside their tents about the travel plans for that day and remember feeling overwhelmed with love for them. All of my previous annoyance at them disappeared and I was able to see them in a new light.

The next month of traveling was a time of increasing joy for me. Together we continued to visit beautiful places and do amazing things, but I no longer felt the need to understand my life. I felt complete. Even though we were a thousand miles away from Pennsylvania, from that moment on I experienced, in every mile that I drove, the feeling that I was already home.

2

SILENCE
Our Greatest Teacher

The greatest experience I have of God is in silence. Even though, as a priest, much of my life is spent talking about God—teaching and explaining God to others and reflecting on the mystery of God—it is silence that provides me with an experience of God that is unique.

At first glance, this way of prayer might not appear like prayer at all. It does not consist of much speaking, thinking, or reading. This way of prayer is more about *being* than anything else. There is no *doing*: no long prayers, petitions, novenas, or reading. When we sit in silence, we are not looking for consolations, insights, answers to difficult questions, or anything else. (Though if God chooses to give them, we can accept them with gratitude.) Instead, we are, quite simply, sitting in silence, or in other words, attempting to rest in him beyond words, ideas, and images.

When I speak about this way of prayer, people often close their eyes as if they were savoring fresh, cold water on a sweltering summer day. When their eyes open they look at me with a smile that seems to say, "This is what I need so desperately." They "need" it for the same reasons I do. We are distracted, noisy, confused, and torn in various directions. We are overwhelmed, anxious, insecure, afraid, and weak in the midst of countless temptations and endless change.

Despite how many spiritual books we read and prayers we recite, this feeling of being tossed about at sea continues to increase. Even though we experience a reprieve at times with insights from Scripture, vocal prayer, the example of the saints, and so on, there is still something more that we need. St. John of the Cross says that "our greatest need is to be silent before this great God with the appetite and with the tongue, for the only language he hears is the silent language of love."[1] Silence before God is not only our greatest need; it is also our greatest teacher.

A few years ago, I realized that no matter how much I read and study, my knowledge and insights are, in the end, limited. It was as if all my talking to God and thinking about God brought me to the edge of a cliff. To get to the other side, I would need something else. That something else, I finally realized, was silence.

I began to follow this inclination toward silence more and more each day. I would sit for fifteen minutes, thirty minutes, sometimes even a whole hour, opening my heart to God alone in silence. When I would get tangled up in my thoughts, I would simply say the name of Jesus or Abba, or recite a short prayer from Scripture, such as "Come, Lord Jesus" (Revelation 22:20), "Speak, LORD, for your servant is listening" (1 Samuel 3:9), or "Draw me after you" (Song of Songs 1:4), so as to bring my attention back to the Lord, with whom I was desiring just to be.

One of the first fruits that we discover from praying in silence is the simple yet profound realization that we are not our thoughts. For almost my entire life I identified my self with my thoughts. If I felt lonely, afraid, or inadequate, then I identified

---

1   Letter 8, in *The Collected Works of St. John of the Cross*, trans. Kieran Kavanaugh and Otilio Rodriguez (Washington, DC: ICS Publications, 1991), 742.

myself with these things. Instead of being a child of God made in his image and likeness, I was whatever my thoughts were telling me simply because they appeared to be true. Silence provides us with the space to discover that our thoughts, like the passing clouds, are simply a facet about us and not our whole self. Beyond them, like the clouds, is a clear blue sky, the presence of God, in whom we discover our real identity.

A second fruit from praying in silence is the discovery of the nearness of God. Even though I knew in my mind that God dwelt inside of me, subconsciously I lived most of my life believing that God was "out there," distant from me. God, in this mindset, is more like an alien, inhabiting some remote galaxy, rather than a loving Father who holds all creation in his hand. Through sitting in silence, we can experience that God does not live far away but is one in whom "we live and move and have our being" (Acts 17:28).

When I reflect on my own relationship with God, and ask myself what I desire, the answer that comes back is very simple: God. I don't want just to think about God or talk about God, as necessary as both of those things are. I *want God*. Without silence, not only do I become a slave to impulsive decisions, fear, competition, inordinate desires, and anxiety, but my perception and experience of God will be, at best, immature. This is because God is ultimately beyond our words, language, and concepts; and silence is a bridge leading to a deeper and more mature relationship with God. In this deepening experience of God in silence we can encounter from the very depths of our being a God who is "gracious and merciful, slow to anger and abounding in steadfast love" (Psalm 145:8) and not the distant, detached, dictator God that we, and our culture, often envision God to be.

Lest I fool myself into thinking I have discovered some mystical secret, the reality is I have discovered nothing new. God has been recommending this way of prayer from the beginning. He says, "Be still, and know that I am God" (Psalm 46:10). In other words, silence leads to intimacy. Perhaps the reason I never heard this before was because I wasn't listening.

3
AWAKENING

Somewhere around the age of fourteen, I became afraid of death. I didn't want to see it, think about it, or discuss it. I ignored it as best as I could. Three years later, despite all my best efforts, it caught up with me: My grandmother died one night peacefully in her sleep at the age of eighty-four with a set of rosary beads next to her bed, which she most likely prayed before slipping away into eternity.

A simple woman, she lived on a farm her entire life. She bore three children, including my mother, and had spent her whole life working hard, going to church, and seeking to unite a family that, as time went on, appeared prone to division.

That morning my sister and I had gone to school, as we did every morning. My mother had walked across the street to Grandmother's farm to make sure she had made it downstairs for breakfast. Even though my grandmother was declining both physically and mentally, she had lost none of her willpower.

When mother walked into Grandmother's house that morning, she immediately knew that something was wrong. Grandmother wasn't downstairs sitting in her rocking chair eating breakfast as usual, and there was no sound of her anywhere throughout the house. Mother imagined the worst, that Grandma had fallen down the stairs, or in the bathroom, and was lying unconscious. But Mom did not find her by the stairs or in the bathroom. She finally looked in Grandma's room, and there she was, lying on her back, hands folded, appearing to be in a very deep sleep. In fact, my mother thought that my grandmother was still sleeping until she moved closer and realized she was not breathing. Grandma had died during the night.

We buried her a few days later at Most Blessed Sacrament Catholic Church in Bally, Pennsylvania, where she had spent her entire life as a parishioner. I can't remember what the priest said during the homily, and I can't remember if anybody in my family cried during the Mass. All I remember is looking at the stained-glass windows in the church, which depicted moments in the life of Christ. There were windows of his passion, from his betrayal, his scourging, and his carrying the cross, to his crucifixion. The last window showed the empty tomb, filled with rays of light shining from every direction.

Before I knew it, I snapped out of my daydreaming because the Mass had finished, and the time had come to take my grandmother to the cemetery. The ceremony at the graveside was brief, probably only ten minutes or so, and soon afterward people began to leave because it started to rain. Suddenly, at this moment, as I was kneeling on the frozen December ground before my grandmother's casket, it hit me. My grandmother was dead. I would never see her again. *Never see her again*, I thought. What did those words mean? Why did they sound so violent to my ears?

As I knelt there on the ground, tears began to fall from my eyes.

Is this all there is? This must be a sick joke, I thought. "Grandma," I cried out, "Grandma!" There was no response. Everything was mocking me: the hard ground, the casket staring me in the face, and the rain falling from the sky. I wanted to run away from this dismal place. But where could I go? I wanted to see my grandmother again and tell her that I love her. But I couldn't. She was gone.

I knelt there for a long time until everything became silent. The ground. The casket. Then the rain stopped, leaving a calm and quiet presence in the air around me. I was not accustomed to such silence, and the weight of it quickly overwhelmed me. I did not address God or even try to speak to him. Kneeling before my grandmother's casket, I was speechless before this incredible mystery while questions rattled through my brain: What is the purpose of life? Why is there suffering? What is death? Where do people go when they die?

All of a sudden I felt as if I had woken up from a dream. These questions opened my eyes to something beyond myself. I was immediately filled with a sense that life has a purpose. I felt that I was hearing or sensing the answers to my sincere questions. These were questions of life and death.

My tears ceased while the sadness in my heart began to dissipate. I looked up at her casket again and I knew that somehow, in some way, my grandmother was alive. A gentle smile began to cover my face. I stood there for a few more minutes trying to understand this sudden change that had occurred in me. It was pointless; my mind had failed me.

I kissed her casket a final time and walked with my parents to the car. As we drove away from the cemetery I didn't feel the need to look back at her grave. I knew, in some mysterious way, that she wasn't there. I pulled out her rosary beads from my pocket and squeezed them in my hand. A new set of tears began to form, but this time, much to my surprise, they were tears of joy.

4
THE MARIAN POSTURE

Many families, at some point in their history, have experienced a certain amount of anxiety due to money. My family, unfortunately, was one of them. When my father was shot in his left shoulder during the Vietnam War, he lost the use of that arm. Without a college degree and able to use only one arm, the odds of his ever finding a well-paying job were slim.

So throughout most of my childhood, my father usually worked two jobs at a time. The best jobs he could find were as a security guard and janitor. Although he was grateful for those jobs, each of them only paid him a little more than the minimum wage. With two young children at home, it was never enough. Money always seemed to disappear before all the bills were paid.

When I was lying in bed at night I would often hear my mother and father discussing financial matters. "How are we going to pay for food this month, their school clothes, the doctor visits?" At the time, I was too young to comprehend the seriousness of not having food or clothes for school, or not being able to go to the doctor. What I do remember, though, from overhearing those conversations, was the anxiety in their voices. Without realizing it, and certainly against the will of my parents, their anxiety found its way into my heart.

Thankfully, I always had food and clothes for school, and was able to go to the doctor when needed. But this early childhood experience left a deep mark within me. Rather than embracing life and looking forward to the future, I grew up afraid. The anxiety I encountered from growing up in a poor family convinced me that I was ill-prepared for life. I felt alone, scared, and lost in a world that, at least from my own experience, appeared to conspire against me.

Whenever I was faced with a challenge, whether in school, sports, or human relationships, I immediately became anxious. Since I already felt ill-prepared, I naturally believed I was incompetent to face all of life's challenges. This anxiety manifested itself through a series of "what if" questions. What if I fail this test? What if I lose the game? What if this person doesn't like me? What if . . . ?

Unfortunately, after my return to the Church, this anxiety did not disappear. Not surprisingly, I brought this attitude with me into religious life. Several weeks before I entered the Franciscans I was again plagued with more questions. What if I can't live in New York City? What if I am called to be a Benedictine monk and not a Franciscan friar? What if I am supposed to get married? These questions, fueled by my inherent anxiety toward life, pestered me throughout my initial stages of formation.

It was during this time that I began to look more deeply at the life of Mary. I found, through the various episodes of Mary's life portrayed in the Gospels, that she, perhaps more than anyone, had the right at times to be anxious. Whether it was at the Annunciation, the Flight into Egypt, or the Crucifixion, Mary was never exempt from the trials and uncertainties of life. In fact, her privileged role in salvation history only thrusts her more deeply into them, as Simeon prophesies to her: "a sword will pierce through your own soul also" (Luke 2:35).

What struck me most by meditating on Mary was how she responded to life. Mary's response to the angel Gabriel at the Annunciation is essentially the same response she uttered her entire life: "Behold, I am the handmaid of the Lord; let it be to me according to your word" (Luke 1:38). Despite the heartache, confusion, and sorrow that accompanied Mary's life, she said yes to everything that God allowed. Intrigued by Mary's disposition, I focused my prayer on how Mary said yes to God's mysterious will.

As I compared my situation to Mary's, I began to notice a fundamental difference. Due to my tendency toward anxiety, I approached almost every situation by asking, What if . . . ? What if I can't do this? What if these people don't like me? What if this situation doesn't work out? These questions created more questions, which led to greater anxiety, causing me to become paralyzed before much of life. Mary, on the other hand, had an entirely different approach. Even though she may have asked, What if . . . ? at certain moments in her life, Mary, I believe, moved forward by asking another question: What is . . . real?

By "What is real?" I mean that we can see how Mary rooted herself in reality: the reality of God's fatherly care. This focus of Mary reminded her, beyond all the twists and turns of life, beyond the darkness and confusion that we all must face at times, that God, as a loving Father, is near, trustworthy, and in control. Regardless of what our minds or hearts might like us to believe, by asking ourselves, What is real? we are reminded that the trials and struggles we have to face in this life do not have to cripple us. Faith, as Mary demonstrates, is a light that penetrates through our darkness, revealing to us that we are not alone.

These insights into Mary brought about a radical change in my mind. Instead of being afraid, I attempted to approach life not by asking, What if . . . ? to every situation I faced, but, as we see from Mary's life, reminding myself of what is real: that God is a loving Father whom I can trust. I began to live more in reality as opposed to all the many "what ifs" that don't really exist.

So, you see, anxiety was once as natural to me as the air we breathe, but I began attempting to let go of it. As I did that, I also felt a bit as if I were swimming upstream. But as I placed my trust more deeply in God's care, slowly but surely a deep peace began to resonate within my soul. Now, I can say, many years later, that the grip anxiety once held on me has loosened significantly. Although I still have to struggle against those feelings and self-questioning moments, at times, Mary reminds me that life flows most gracefully when I imitate her faith and trust more fully in God.

5
SOMETHING MORE
A Vocation Story

I was never able to remain in crowds. In elementary school, as soon as the bell rang for recess, students were off like a pack of dogs chasing a ball onto the playground. A quiet country field became a spectacle of childhood games. I, too, was like the rest of the kids, excited to do something, anything, after almost dying of boredom from the morning classes. The excitement for me, however, was short-lived. After playing kickball for a few minutes, I would often leave the game, sit against the wall, and gaze up at the sky.

By the time I was a senior in high school, it seemed we were all obsessed with scoring high on the SATs, visiting our favorite colleges, attracting the opposite sex, and embracing the latest trend. Our frantic attempts and failures at self-realization awoke in me a hunger for something more. I began reading books of poetry, philosophy, religion, and literature, and writing about my desire to see reality in its purest light, rather than live behind a wall of shadows. While reading and writing I felt like a child again, in the presence of a loving parent who was inviting me to explore this road less traveled.

After graduating from college, everyone I knew went in one of three different directions: sending out résumés for jobs, applying to graduate schools, or preparing for marriage and family life. Of these three, the only one I considered seriously was graduate school for either writing or philosophy. I realized, however, the only reason I would choose graduate school was to make myself more appealing to future employers, something that was not bad, but something I was not ultimately interested in. In the middle of this relative confusion, I would often visit the nearest church, where I could be alone in the presence of the Blessed Sacrament to think and to pray, but mostly to listen. There I often felt like I was in a dream in which everyone was sleepwalking, and this mysterious presence was inviting me to wake everyone up. Enlightened by this presence, I chose another path. I gave up everything I owned and moved to New York City to begin living a life of poverty, chastity, and obedience.

Looking back, the way I understand my vocation to religious life is the desire for something more. A part of me was attracted to the same things my friends were: marriage, a career, a family, and the many other good things of the world. For me, the problem with those other options is that they were not enough. When I sat in prayer, and I imagined a "normal" life, I knew immediately that that would not satisfy me.

Some of my more idealistic and philosophically oriented friends understood my vocation to be a social protest against capitalism and a heroic decision to fight for the rights and protection of the poor so as to eradicate human poverty. Even now, after many years of living with the poor, I still chuckle when I think about their misunderstanding of my vocation. Who did they think I was after all? By entering religious life I wasn't protesting or fighting anything or anyone. I didn't choose religious life in anger against the government or social conditions, but to joyfully follow him "who is and who was and who is to come, the Almighty" (Revelation 1:8).

Every Christian, by virtue of baptism, is called to follow in the footsteps of Jesus. What is unique about religious life is that it attempts to be radical by denying those other more common options. The ideal of vowed religious life is not admiring Jesus from a distance, or even walking hand in hand beside him (as the greetings cards sometimes put it). It is complete discipleship, following the Master not only where he goes, but how he lived while on earth. Hence, religious life is sometimes referred to as the "perfect imitation" of Christ. Perfect, not because those living religious life are perfect, but because the way of life they are choosing is the exact life the Son of Man lived while on earth. Through the vows of poverty, chastity, and obedience the vowed religious person is meant to radically imitate Christ in how they live (see John 4:35; Luke 9:58). Like Jesus, the religious chooses poverty for the sake of becoming rich in what matters to God. He chooses chastity for the sake of a greater love. And he chooses obedience because he wishes to be led ultimately by the Father.

I know: not every vowed religious person does these things. We have seen that all too clearly in recent days in the Church. Father, forgive us! I also know that laypeople who do not take vows of poverty, chastity, and obedience, but rather have careers and create families, can be more like Jesus in their hearts and lives than those of us who are priests, monks, friars, and sisters.

In a culture that is obsessed with sex, status, and material possessions, vowed religious people, and every person of sincere and true faith who is living in God's will for their lives, are to be a prophetic sign pointing to something more. If you are married, your love for your spouse must be pure, holy, and life-giving. If you are a person in power or authority over others, know that there is a higher law, and that God's ways are the true path that leads to human freedom. If you are in doubt or questioning the faith, remember to consider, to probe deeper into your heart, and discover the one "who forms the mountains, and creates the wind . . . who makes the morning darkness, and treads on the heights of the earth—the LORD, the God of hosts, is his name" (Amos 4:13).

It has been sixteen years since I left everything to follow Jesus. In that time, I have lived a full life. I have been ordained a priest; preached all over the world; buried my own mother; spent endless hours with the homeless, prostitutes, drug addicts, and those suffering from mental illness; spent days and weeks alone with God in a hermitage; and lived in places I would have never imagined, like Harlem, Newark, Texas, and New Mexico.

Yet the most remarkable aspect of my life is the growing intimacy I experience with Jesus as I stumble along each day following in his footsteps. Poverty, chastity, and obedience have purified me, humbled me, strengthened me, and forced me to "seek the things that are above" (Colossians 3:1).

Religious life certainly is not perfect. The rules and customs can seem outdated, too idealistic, and even inhuman at times. Sometimes my fear, pride, or stubbornness prevents me from simply being led "where [I] do not wish to go" (John 21:18). The people in religious life struggle with human problems like depression, fear, scrupulosity, self-hate, and insecurity. Even our superiors sometimes give commands that are not based on reason or even good discernment but on their own brokenness. Through this imperfect reality one is given the opportunity to follow in the footsteps of Jesus, who "was oppressed, and

. . . afflicted" (Isaiah 53:7), "despised and rejected by men . . . wounded for our transgressions, [and] bruised for our iniquities" (Isaiah 53:3, 5).

Despite my struggles with broken humanity, I have never once considered leaving religious life. Why would I? It has always lived up to its promise of leading me to something more. I have discovered a treasure in a field, and like the man in the parable "in his joy he goes and sells all that he has and buys that field" (Matthew 13:44). Yet as I grow older I am becoming increasingly aware there is still more of God, more human experiences, more life that I have yet to encounter. I still feel at times like a child, fascinated by the simplest discovery, yet far away from perfect maturity. Currently, I am living a more contemplative expression of Franciscan life, one that includes large periods of silence and solitude. The reason is not because I want to avoid people, but because I am falling more deeply in love with the silent presence of God, who is continuing to invite me, even in this desire, to still something more.

I invite you, religious or nonreligious, to do this too. Live this adventure in your life. With God, there is always more.

6
SURPRISED BY GRACE

As soon as the phone rang my heart began to race. Something told me this would not be a regular phone call.

"Hello," I said, hesitantly.

"Father," said a woman's voice. "This is a miracle. My cousin wants to see a priest. I have been praying for this day for years. Can you visit him?"

"Okay," I said, somewhat cautiously. "What kind of visit is he looking for? Does he want to go to confession, is he sick, or does he just want to speak with a priest?"

"I'm not exactly sure," she said. "But this is a miracle."

"Well then, I would be happy to visit him," I said. "Where does your cousin live?"

"Well," she said, followed by a brief pause, "he is in prison."

As a priest, I thought, I have seen and heard it all. After hearing thousands of confessions and spending many hours in spiritual direction with people, I find it difficult to be shocked or surprised by what anyone says or does. I had recently told a friend that for me, as a priest, there are no more surprises. Yet after I hung up the phone with this woman, I began to realize that perhaps I was wrong.

It is not uncommon of course for a priest to visit people in prison. However, in my years as a priest, prison had been one of the places I had never been sent before. Perhaps like most people,

I had an image in my mind, not only of what prison was like, but also of what the prisoners themselves were like. Unfortunately, I imagined prison to be a place filled with hardened criminals who had no concern for people. I supposed that the majority of people in prison had little if any faith in God, and most, I believed, were not interested in the spiritual life. There was a part of me, I am ashamed to admit, that was wondering if I was wasting my time by making this visit.

When I arrived at the prison, I stood outside my car and stared in wonder at what looked like a giant fortress. After spending almost thirty minutes trying to find the entrance, I entered the visitor's section only to spend another thirty minutes going through security. Finally, I was allowed to enter a large room, which looked like a dining hall, where several other inmates were visiting with their own guests. At each corner of the room stood several armed guards, surveying the room and checking to see if each visitor was wearing the proper pass that allowed him into the designated area.

I sat down at the table assigned to me by the guard and waited. After a long wait, the man I was asked to visit appeared and sat down at my table. He was not anything like I expected. Rather than shaking my hand, he immediately hugged me and expressed how grateful he was that I would take the time to visit him. As he began to speak, I was shocked at his demeanor. Instead of being angry, rude, and tough like I expected, he was quiet, calm, and polite.

"Father," he said, with a tear beginning to form in his eye, "in prison I met Jesus Christ."

He paused, waiting for me to respond. "I wasn't expecting that to be your opening line," I said, while smiling at him. We both laughed so hard that we caught the attention of the guards, who looked at us with suspicion. After regaining our composure he spent the next few moments sharing with me how he ended up in prison and all that had occurred to him during his time there. As he finished, he looked down at the ground for a few seconds and appeared lost in deep thought.

"Father, I have accepted God's mercy and I believe in his love for me despite the terrible things I have done. I am hungry, Father, and I want to know more. How do I pray? Can you teach me about the Bible? Why are the sacraments important?" I looked at him in amazement. Immediately I thought of Jesus's words to the centurion in Matthew 8:10, "Not even in Israel have I found such faith."

I spent the next hour attempting to answer his questions. As I spoke he stared at me in awe, as if his life made sense for the first time. Occasionally, a tear rolled down his face, forcing me to fight back my own. Suddenly I realized that the man before me was not the person I had imagined him to be. Yes, he had done some horrible things and he deserved to be in prison. But now he was different. The power of God's mercy had transformed this man into someone new, someone his friends, and especially those whom he hurt, probably would not recognize.

As I drove home that afternoon, I reflected on my conversation with this man and thought to myself, "This is what redemption looks like." Redemption, after all, is not something we can do. Despite our good intentions and best efforts we always remain in need of a Savior. St. Paul reminds us, "All have sinned and fall short of the glory of God," but "they are justified by his grace as a gift, through the redemption which is in Christ Jesus" (Romans 3:23–24).

The man I met in prison is proof that redemption is possible. For years, he had followed his own way, without any regard for a higher law. Rather than bring him the freedom he desired, his selfishness imprisoned him. Ironically, it was there, amid such darkness and pain, that the light of God's mercy opened his eyes, removed his chains, and set him free.

NOT ENOUGH

I have this insatiable thirst for God. In the morning, after beginning a time of solitary prayer, a quiet presence reveals itself in my heart, inviting me to rest without words or ideas. By evening, this presence I met so peacefully in prayer has become a wildfire that burns and brightens with each moment. Each activity, conversation, and thought only increases its vigor. The longer I live, it seems, the stronger it becomes. It is impossible to extinguish.

I return to this thirst again and again.

Sometimes when I visit a new place I wonder what life would be like living here. I daydream about its mountains, its lakes, its people, or its small towns, and I imagine myself living there devoid of problems and annoyances. I think that living here, in this place, I could be perfectly happy and content. Yet as time goes by, I realize that this place, in all its wonder and beauty, is not the ultimate place where my heart can rest. It is, after all, limited.

Sometimes when I meet a new person I can get lost in the excitement of their presence. What insights will they reveal to me about myself, what experiences will I share with them that can help me feel more fulfilled, or even what material gifts might they give me to enable me to enjoy life more fully? If the benefits are great, I can begin to think that the reason my life was "lacking" before was because this person was absent from my life. Yet, as time goes by, I realize that this person, despite being a blessing, is, like me, limited.

Sometimes when I am engaged in apostolic work, whether it is preaching or serving the homeless, I can begin to think that if only I could do what I felt called to when I want and how I feel called to do it, I would no longer become frustrated or disappointed with life. The reason, of course, for my frustration is because my superiors, my family, and my friends don't understand the gifts God has given me. Or so I think. Yet, as time goes by, and when I have the opportunity to do what I want, when I want, and how I want to do it, and even call it "God's will," I realize that all of this, with all of its certitude and applause, is still limited.

Speaking of the human heart the prophet Jeremiah says, "Who can understand it?" (Jeremiah 17:9). Though I would never raise my hand and say, "I do," there is one thing that I do know about my own heart: it is thirsting. My heart is thirsting for something beyond rest, affirmation, comfort, prestige, popularity, and anything else that this world can give. Of all the foolish decisions I have made in my life perhaps the most foolish one is thinking, and even expecting, that some "thing" of this world can satisfy me.

A helpful comparison to understand just how silly this endeavor is would be to compare it to trying to empty out the ocean with a bucket. Something that big, the ocean (our human heart), can never be captured by something as small as a bucket (this world). The problem lies in the vast differences of size. One is large, spacious, and seemingly infinite, while the other is small, rigid, and finite. Yet even though I recognize the utter stupidity of such an attempt, I would say we continue to try.

The dilemma is not that rest, friendship, our own gifts and talents, or anything else of this world is bad; but they can never satisfy us completely. God, in his great mercy, never allows us to experience complete fulfillment in this world. He keeps inspiring us to go beyond this transitory world in which everything is vulnerable and exposed to change and to embrace the One who "laid the foundation of the earth" (Job 38:4), who "was in the beginning," through whom "all things were made" (John 1:2–3), and whose "years have no end" (Psalm 102:27).

I do this not when I abandon the world but when I receive this world as a gift. I try to allow all the world's joys and beauties to take me beyond it to the One in whom I can find a permanent resting place. If God has allowed me a certain amount of success in my ministry or if I am fortunate enough to spend a few days in a beautiful location, I must view these gifts not as ends in themselves, but as a further means to increasing my desire for the One who gave them. This is why I say that I have an insatiable thirst for God, because, despite the glamor and promises of this world, no matter where I travel, who I meet, and what I do, in the end it is simply not enough.

8
ENCOUNTERING WEAKNESS

I realize that most people don't preach, nor perhaps do they want to. But preaching is an essential part of Franciscan life, and it is a big part of my life.

When St. Francis encountered the love of God in Jesus Christ his life was radically altered. Almost overnight Francis went from a man of this world to one in pursuit of the things of heaven. He traded in his fancy clothes for those of a poor beggar. He said goodbye to his earthly father, who could not accept his son's transformation, and embraced God as his Father. He abandoned his middle-class Italian life, with all its pleasures and luxuries, and went to live with lepers and those estranged from society.

St. Francis did all of this, not because of political or economic motivations, but because he wanted to imitate Jesus, who "emptied himself, taking the form of a servant" (Philippians 2:7). Francis's desire was simple: to live the gospel and share with the world that "pearl of great price" he had received. The rich, the poor, young, old, and even animals listened to this "troubadour of the Lord," as he went about proclaiming the gospel to all of creation. The whole world was not only his cloister but also his audience.

But preaching is not merely a Franciscan way of life—in a way, it's an essential part of the life of any Christian. When I first heard the gospel, it was like fresh spring water washing over me. It was purifying, refreshing, and humbling. For some time, I simply bathed in those waters, not trying to understand, but just enjoying its freshness and vigor. Fairly soon, however, I realized, this good news was not meant only for me. I needed to share it. Once we discover the joy of the good news, we know that we can't keep it for ourselves.

Like St. Paul, I believe "an obligation has been imposed on me, and woe to me if I do not preach it" (1 Corinthians 9:16 NAB). Whether it is a retreat, a parish mission, a day of recollection, or some other preaching event, I am generally excited and anxious to share what I believe is the heart of the gospel: that no matter who you are, where you are from, or what you have done, God is deeply in love with you. Jesus is the proof.

Anyone who has attempted to share the gospel knows it is not easy. Perhaps I am a bit naïve, but every time I venture out to proclaim this message I expect a smooth takeoff. Within moments, however, I encounter turbulence.

Aside from traffic jams, car problems, flight delays, and stomach pains, there are the deeper disturbances to contend with. First, there's what I like to call "mind turbulence." It begins with questions: *Why am I preaching here? Why did I choose this topic? Did I really discern this properly? Are my talks too long, too short? Are they too theological? Does anybody care about what I'm saying?* Next comes an endless array of thoughts plagued with doubt and insecurity. *Nobody is going to come. The pastor thinks I'm too young. I shouldn't have left my hermitage. I'm such a hypocrite; I shouldn't be preaching on something I'm not living.*

Then, there is the "environmental turbulence." Like clockwork, as soon as I arrive for the event something goes wrong with the sound system, electricity, air conditioner, or heater. Coupled with that is a whole group of enthusiastic people waiting to tell me their hopes and their expectations for the event. Somewhere inside this crowd there is that one person who does not hesitate to tell me everything that is wrong with this place, its people, its pastor, its programs, and that my being there, despite good intentions, will not really change anyone.

By this point my head is usually spinning, my stomach is in pain, and I am convinced this event will be a disaster. Clearly this cannot be God's will. I turn to prayer for confirmation. There is no consolation, no affirmation, and no sense of God's presence. If God does "speak" to me in these moments, it is often with the same words he gave to St. Paul in the midst of his own struggles he encountered in proclaiming the gospel: "My grace is sufficient for you, for my power is made perfect in weakness" (2 Corinthians 12:9).

When the time has arrived to begin preaching I approach the microphone with a deep awareness of my own poverty. I have been completely stripped. I have no confidence, no wisdom, and no strength. I am not exactly sure what I will say or how I will say it. I feel alone. I open my mouth and suddenly it happens: everything disappears. The turbulence ceases, and I feel, quite literally, as if I am floating, being carried by a Presence much stronger than anything of this world. Somehow the words flow in a way my audience can understand. The gospel, despite any turbulence, is being proclaimed, and strangely enough, I am its messenger.

St. Paul reminds us, "When I am weak, then I am strong" (2 Corinthians 12:10). Be encouraged in your own ministry when you become overwhelmed by your inadequacies. God can do a lot with nothing, if you are willing to surrender even that to him. St. Francis stripped himself of his clothes to become utterly dependent on God. I, too, when I preach, am stripped of any self-reliance. Each time, I learn again the same message: God's grace transforms our weakness.

9
MARTHA'S GIFT

As a child, I would go for long walks in the woods behind my house to be alone with God. In those solitary woods, among a vast array of natural beauty, the presence of God was as ordinary to me as the air. The trees, animals, and lakes were a reflection of a reality much greater than this world. What fascinated me was not the forest itself, but the Creator of such magnificent scenes. Though I did not utter many prayers in those woods, I went there to simply be with God, which, I would learn much later, is the real essence of prayer.

After dinner, when I was no longer able to roam about outside, I felt compelled to try to articulate what I encountered in those solitary moments with nature. Curiously, the attempt to write about my own experience was almost as exciting and beautiful as the experience itself. Writing, for me, was a process of discovery. Even though I had felt something, heard something, or seen something, it wasn't until I wrote about it that I came to a clearer understanding of how near God was to me.

Both writing and prayer have consumed a significant amount of time and energy in my life. When prayer is consoling me and writing is nourishing me I feel alive and eager to share my joy with everyone around me. Yet when prayer is dry and I am unable to express my thoughts in words, I often feel frustrated and want to isolate myself from the rest of the world. This is why I've vowed, at times, to quit one of these activities, so as to focus exclusively on the other, only to find myself a few days later plunging more deeply into both of them than ever before.

On the surface, writing and prayer can appear to be two different activities. However, I am discovering a surprising symmetry between them. Writing, I have come to realize, is my Martha, while prayer is my Mary. In the Gospel of Luke there is a famous episode where Jesus enters the home of Martha and Mary. Mary sits at his feet and listens to him, while Martha is busy serving and taking care of the practical needs of her guest. Frustrated by her sister's apparent laziness, Martha complains to Jesus and asks him to support her. Jesus responds, "Martha, Martha, you are anxious and worried about many things. There is need of only one thing. Mary has chosen the better part and it will not be taken from her" (Luke 10:41–42 NAB).

We can often view the activity of our life, whether it is our job, family, or social responsibilities, as a distraction from the "better part" that Mary chose. What we often fail to recognize is that our activity often prepares the way, both for ourselves and others, for this silent receptivity that Mary exemplifies. Without Martha's activity Mary wouldn't be free to sit at Jesus's feet. Mary herself was not free from daily responsibilities. It was only by fulfilling them that she was able to receive Jesus with such reverent attention.

I am beginning to understand my relationship with writing and prayer in a similar fashion. I have often wondered what purpose my writing serves as a Franciscan priest and have been tempted to quit writing because of my inability to see how it relates to my vocation. I have entertained the notion that writing is a distraction, preventing me from deeper intimacy with God, and that if I just quit writing, I would be holier because I could devote more time to prayer, meditation, and preaching. Within the past few months I have discovered not only that writing is an expression of my love for Jesus, but also that without it, I could not sit quietly at his feet and listen. In other words, without Martha I cannot be Mary.

There is a misconception among certain people that those who live in monasteries, convents, or friaries sit around and just pray all day. My own sister often tells her friends, "I'm not really sure what my brother does all day!" Despite the fact that religious have times reserved for prayer, meditation, and spiritual exercises, when we are not engaged in those pursuits we live a normal human life, a life filled with activity. Even though God loves us and cares for us, he does not cook our food, clean our homes, or answer our doorbell.

I know that this activity is not a distraction in my relationship with God. On the contrary, it is the activity of the day that opens my heart and creates in me a longing for God. As I sit in prayer in the morning with the duties and the responsibilities of the day staring in front of me, I become aware of my need for God's grace before I approach these tasks. When nighttime arrives, with the activity of the day behind me, my heart and mind are more disposed toward quiet contemplation, as I ponder the many ways I encountered God that day.

Perhaps Martha's fault was not her activity, but her inability to see how her activity was meant to be a bridge to something greater. The activity of our life, whether it is writing or anything else, is never an end in itself. What Mary has to teach each of us, I think, and what I am learning through my writing, is that our work in this life is never complete. If it were, we would never experience the deep peace that comes from simply resting at the feet of Jesus.

THE ONE THING

Even though five years have passed, I can remember the moment as if it were yesterday. It was a typical morning in Harlem. The phone rang every five minutes and the doorbell every ten. I was meeting individually with postulants, the youngest members of my community, and listening to their struggles with prayer, celibacy, fraternal living, and leaving their family. Outside the streets were rowdy: car horns, street-cleaning machines, rap music, and our neighbor Linda who has schizophrenia, cursing and laughing as she walked up and down the street.

Savoring a brief moment of silence after meeting with one of the postulants, I whispered, "Where are you Lord?" I will sometimes do this—talk aloud to God, particularly when I feel overwhelmed, tired, or incompetent to do what God seems to be asking of me. Mostly, though, I was frustrated at that moment. In the tense environment in which I found myself, religious life wasn't what I had expected.

Where was the romance of it all? My vocation wasn't turning out to be as I had thought it would be. Jesus told his disciples that whoever "would come after me, let him deny himself and take up his cross daily and follow me" (Luke 9:23). Surely those words didn't apply to me, now, in this situation, did they? How could they?

"Fr. Jeremiah," a brother's voice spoke over the intercom, "a woman is on the phone who would like to talk to a priest."

Sure, I thought to myself. *Everyone wants to talk to a priest, as if we have all the answers.* "Thank you," I responded. "I'll be right there."

Before I even finished saying hello she began. "I recently went to a parish mission . . . I have been away from church for years . . . I haven't been praying . . . I realize that my life is empty, and I am frustrated." And then she said it: "I want to know who God is."

Suddenly she had my full attention. The noise from outside disappeared. The self-pity I was entertaining vanished, and the burden I was experiencing from my responsibilities lifted. I was fascinated by her last sentence. "I want to know who God is." It sounded so familiar.

For a brief moment, I had a flashback to elementary school when I was an altar boy at Mass. This particular morning there were only about fifteen people in church, each varying in age, ethnicity, and social status. There was no singing, no large crowds, no long sermons. We listened to the Scriptures, prayed, sat together in silence, and knelt humbly as the priest held up bread and wine. The whole time I stood next to the priest, unable to comprehend the moment, but feeling myself being drawn into another world.

After Mass as I was walking over to school I stopped and said to myself, "I want to know who God is." I thought, even then, *Where did those words come from?* Although I had just come from church I wasn't thinking anything particularly spiritual. I think I was trying to remember if I had completed my homework, and what time baseball practice was that day. Yet those words, *I want to know who God is*, echoed within me.

A few seconds later the flashback faded, along with all the other distractions I was living in. Something had woken up inside of me.

"Does this make any sense?" she asked, sounding desperate for affirmation.

"Yes," I said, as a tear began to take shape in my eye. "I think I understand." We were both silent for a few moments.

"Would you like to get together so we can talk?" I calmly asked her.

"Yes," she said. "When are you available?"

As we scheduled a time for our appointment and hung up the phone, I stood there repeating her words, "I want to know who God is." A childlike grin came over my face as I laughed out loud.

"Of course," I said to myself. "What else is there?"

11
ORIGINAL DESIRE

When I was sixteen years old I wanted it all: to be athletic, intelligent, strong, attractive, genuine, funny, articulate, and a whole lot more.

Every one of these desires demanded my full attention. They were the epitome of selfishness. Depending on the day, I would start with the one directly in front of me—in other words, whichever was shouting the loudest. To be athletic, I would throw myself into training like an Olympic athlete, organizing every moment of my day around improving the sport I was currently obsessed with. To be attractive I would examine all my faults, both physical and mental, and devise a plan, effective immediately, on how to eradicate my imperfections.

By the time I was nineteen, I made another important discovery: my desires never quit. If I "conquered" one, whether it was a sport, a book, an exterior quality, or whatever, there would be another lurking in the shadows, begging to be noticed. If I could master throwing a curveball, why not master throwing a slider and a changeup as well? If I read everything by Ernest Hemingway (because, surely, doing so would make me a writer the world would admire), why not read everything by John Steinbeck or F. Scott Fitzgerald also?

When any one of these desires began to take shape inside my heart, it was as if a voice from some mysterious place whispered, "I am what you need. If you possess, me you will be complete."

I honestly believed each of them was like a key, and if I could attain that key, it would open up for me the happiness, peace, and serenity I longed for. It took me many years to realize an important component to this game: there is no end. One either has to quit, which I believe is impossible, or go beyond these desires, to what I like to call our original desire.

A few weeks ago, I was speaking with a childhood friend, somebody who watched me pursue these desires day after day. Unlike me, he didn't feel like his life needed an explanation. In fact, he believed there was no explanation. Life was just life, nothing more. These desires were random occurrences due mostly to our social conditioning and genetic makeup. After an hour or so of philosophical and theological debate together he simply asked me, "What then is the greatest thing Jesus has done in your life?" Without hesitation I said, "He has organized my heart."

Ever since the fall of Adam the human heart has been disorganized. The answer is not just having all the necessary parts but having them in their proper place. The strange thing is that we often hide, or at least attempt to hide, from the only One who can bring order out of our chaos. "They heard the sound of the LORD God walking in the garden in the cool of the day, and the man and his wife hid themselves from the presence of the LORD God among the trees of the garden" (Genesis 3:8).

This hiding on our part forces God to ask, "Where are you?" (Genesis 3:9). Despite Adam and Eve's cleverness, and ours, God has not lost sight of them, or of us. We have lost sight of God. The question is meant to provoke in us a realization: there is only One who "formed my inward parts," who "knitted me together in my mother's womb . . . when I was being made in secret," and whose "eyes beheld my unformed substance" (Psalm 139:13–16). In other words, God is the source of the human heart, and every desire, despite all its allure and glamour, is only a pointer back to that one, true original desire, which is communion with its source.

As I began to read the New Testament and open my heart to Jesus, this reality for me "took flesh." At first I was like the tax collector in the parable who "would not even lift up his eyes to heaven, but beat his breast, saying 'God, be merciful to me a sinner'" (Luke 18:13). Fairly soon, however, after experiencing God's mercy so deeply, my prayer became a gaze fixed on the person of Jesus, and I too "sat at the Lord's feet and listened to his teaching" (Luke 10:39). This love that I encountered in Jesus began to consume my heart, pushing everything else, including those pesky desires, away from my heart's center. What I once didn't even know was possible was slowly beginning to occur: my heart was becoming organized.

I desperately want this for every person I encounter.

As our hearts become organized, it's not that our various desires are extinguished. But it means they're put in their proper place. I think many of us hope, at least subconsciously, that our desires will reveal us to ourselves. In other words, we want them to tell us who we are, because whether we like it or not, we cannot escape from our heart's restless pursuit of that answer. I found in my own pursuits that being strong, athletic, smart, outgoing, articulate, and funny wasn't enough. Finally, after much hesitation, I heeded the words of Jesus: "Come to me, all who labor and are heavy laden, and I will give you rest . . . for I am gentle and lowly in heart, and you will find rest for your souls" (Matthew 11:28–29).

What did Jesus show me? Namely, that he is my desire. The point of our desires, I believe, is to reveal to us something greater, something beyond this world of space and time that contains not only our origin but also our destiny. Regardless of who we are and where we have come from, nothing else satisfies.

FORTY DAYS
(BEFORE)

When I was in college, most of my summers were spent living in my car. My friends and I would work as much as possible to earn enough money to live off for a few weeks. As soon as we had enough we would quit, only to begin another journey whose destination was unknown to us. The thrill of the open road and the promises they whispered to us were too much of a temptation. We surrendered every time.

The point of traveling, I thought, was not necessarily to *see* something new, but to *experience* something new. This experience, more than just an emotion, was meant to alter one's worldview, and give new meaning to life.

When I entered the Franciscans, I thought my traveling days were over, only to realize that in some ways they had just begun. For my first assignment after making temporary vows, I was assigned to be one of four friars on an experimental "mission team" whose purpose was to travel the world preaching the gospel. Instead of jumping into my car, I was now boarding a plane, and similar to my experience in college, I often did not know where I was going.

But I don't only preach. In fact, in just a few weeks, I will embark on what is truly the longest journey of my life. For it, I will not need a car or a plane; I will not need money or places to stay. I will not be preaching retreats or giving spiritual direction. I will be spending forty days alone in a hermitage.

✳   ✳   ✳

In Christianity, solitude has always been considered, not as an escape from reality, but as a journey into its very heart. After Christianity became legal in the fourth century, there was a group of Christians who feared that the legalization of their religion could water down their faith. Terrified at this notion, these men and women, known as the Desert Fathers and Mothers, abandoned the comfort that a legalized religion brought, and entered the wild and unchartered land of the desert. Their goal, like all true solitaries, was not to escape life, but to live in direct contact with its source.

Those hermits did not create something new, but walked in ancient footsteps. St. John the Baptist, St. Paul, and even our Lord spent an extensive period of solitude in the desert. In fact, it was from this time in solitude that their ministry emerged. Even earlier, God told Israel through Hosea,

> I will allure her,
> and bring her in the wilderness,
> and speak tenderly to her. (Hosea 2:14)

When God leads Israel out of Egypt into the desert she is confused, afraid, and lost. Despite God's nearness to her and his constant saving help, Moses tells the Israelites, "You did not believe the LORD your God, who went before you in the way to seek out a place to pitch your tents" (Deuteronomy 1:32–33). Ancient Israel's faith was childish. They only believed in what they could see and cling to. Since all they knew was slavery in Egypt, that is all they could imagine their lives to be. Perhaps the reason they ended up spending not just forty days but forty years in the desert was because it took them that long to let go of narrow and limited ways of thinking, before they could embrace the expansive vision God had planned for them.

About four years ago I spent two weeks in a hermitage in South Texas. For most of that time I was alone, without the comfort of friends, my community, or a familiar landscape. When people asked me what I did during that time I responded, "I mostly listened." What occurred in that listening is difficult to express in words. One way I have described those two weeks is by referring to it as a "second conversion" experience. In that desert, stripped of everything that was familiar, I met the living God whom I thought I already knew.

Shortly after my time in South Texas, I received the inspiration to spend forty days in hermitage. Like ancient Israel, I have struggled to know where God is leading me. After all, I belong to a very active religious community, in which the overwhelming majority is moving not toward the desert, but deeper into the city. Though I admire this work, the Spirit appears to be moving me in an opposite direction, causing me to ask, *God, is this really you, and if so, what are you saying to me?*

As my time to enter the desert again draws near, I wish I felt confident and unafraid. What I will encounter on this next journey I do not know. Yet in many ways, the "what" is the least important. One goes to the desert not for an experience, but to answer a call. This call has led me to the Red Sea, as the waters begin to open.

13
HEROIC LOVE

My mother spent the last fifteen years of her life in a nursing home suffering from Alzheimer's disease. I would be a liar if I said that her disease had not caused my family much suffering or that we accepted it perfectly as part of God's mysterious will. The reality is, we all suffered and we all questioned how God could allow this to happen to somebody each one of us desperately needed.

An unfortunate consequence of Alzheimer's is that a person's brain actually shrinks. As the years went by, my mother's mental state became similar to that of a child. The hard-working, intelligent, and nurturing woman I knew as a boy had disappeared. Physically she looked the same, but when I looked into her eyes I saw a little girl who appeared lost and was trying to find her way home.

When I arrived at the nursing home for a visit all she talked about was going outside to smoke a cigarette. As soon as we were outside, all she talked about was going back inside, and vice versa for the whole duration of the visit, which for me never exceeded three hours, but for my father was often all afternoon. After a few months, I gave up hope of hearing her say she was glad to see me, because, I realized, my mother was no longer present.

On certain days, she would yell and curse and call the nurses names. In the beginning they would laugh and approach her with a friendly smile, but as the months dragged on and the insults continued they became tired, annoyed, and avoided her as best they could. After only a month or two of working at the nursing home, a new employee quickly learned that my mother was considered one of the "difficult" patients.

Despite all this, my father continued to visit her every day. He walked into her room, gave her a kiss, and brought her outside in her wheelchair to smoke. Once outside he would face the same barrage of questions he answered the day before. "How long have we been married?" "Is Fr. Jeremiah married?" "How much money did I make last year?" "When are they going to feed me?" "What is Tammy's husband's name again?" After listening to these questions for hours my father would wheel her back inside her room, kiss her again, and return to his home, alone.

Occasionally, my father got mad and expressed his frustration in words that would have been better left unspoken. These words, I believe, came from a place of mourning and frustration, as he was forced to watch the woman he loved deteriorate in front of him and not be able to do anything about it. Not only had my mother become helpless because of her disease, but also now my father was experiencing his own poverty, as he stood before my mom helpless.

Thirty years ago, my father promised to love my mother "for better or for worse, in sickness and in health, and to love and cherish her until death do us part." Could he ever have imagined what those vows would ask of him? Would he still have made them knowing what he knows now? Rather than spending his days entertaining abstract questions, my father did something I consider heroic: he was obedient to reality. By choosing to live in reality and not escape through endless speculations of "what if," "why me," or worse, he proved his love for his wife.

Watching my father through all of this revealed to me an essential component of love: it is utterly selfless. So often we reduce love to a feeling or an experience of pleasure, yet St. Paul reminds us, "Love does not insist on its own way" (1 Corinthians 13:5). When my father would slip and allow his frustrations to control his actions, he would begin again the next day where he left off, at my mother's side.

If I or anybody else would ever tell my dad that his fidelity to his wife was heroic, he would probably look at you as if you were speaking a foreign language. "It's what love does," he would probably say. "I had no other choice." The reality is, he did have a choice. He could have chosen one of many escape paths: despair, resignation, anger, or any number of ways that the world tells us to dull our pain or distract us for a few moments. Despite the allure they may have possessed, my father chose none of them.

At my mother's funeral, I read these words of Jesus in the Gospel: "Greater love has no man than this, that a man lay down his life for his friends" (John 15:13). When I heard those words at Mass a deep sense of peace and gratitude came over me. I was peaceful because I believed in the depths of my heart that Jesus's love, selfless and sacrificial, conquered death. I was grateful because it was my father who showed me what this looked like.

14
AUTHENTICITY

Over the years, I have spoken to many people about their relationship with God. In many ways, that's what I do.

I find that everyone, on some level, desires to know the secret of holiness, even if they don't use those words. If they are young, they often imagine that holiness involves some magnificent feat of strength or courage, perhaps engaging in disciplined asceticism or undergoing some form of persecution. If they are older, they think that holiness involves hours of undistracted prayer, followed by self-sacrifice devoid of anger or resentment. If the person is a priest or a religious, their standard of holiness is often measured by fidelity to their vocation. If one is faithful to their vows and fulfilling perfectly the rules and norms of their vocation, then holiness is a natural consequence.

After each person has defended his view with sound reasoning, orthodox theology, and examples from the lives of the saints, I feel the need to interject.

"Everything you said is true," I usually say, "but you are missing an important point. If you really want to be holy, all the things you mentioned can be helpful, but . . . they must be authentic. Most importantly, *you* must be authentic."

A mixture of surprise and confusion usually begins to appear on their face as they stare at the ground for a few moments.

"What does authenticity have to do with holiness?" they ask sincerely.

"Everything!" I almost shout.

Asceticism, deep prayer, and fidelity to one's vocation are all necessary means to holiness, yet before these aspects of our spiritual life begin, they must be born from an authentic place. Authenticity means, first and foremost, being the person God has created you to be. In order for that to happen, we must always return to the foundational question: Who am I before God? In other words, we must consider things like our personality, cultural background, and talents as we attempt to respond to Jesus's call to discipleship. The reason for this is simple. It is through our own humanity, never somebody else's, that we will encounter God and be able to respond to him appropriately.

For example, Jesus recommends "prayer and fasting" (Mark 9:29) as a necessary component of our spiritual lives. However, the prayer and fasting of a twenty-year-old is going to look very different from that of a seventy-year-old. Likewise, the prayer and fasting of someone who is sick will look different from that of one who is healthy. Which person is praying and fasting better? The one who is responding most fully to the grace God is giving him. The one who is most authentic.

The best examples of authentic holiness can be found, unsurprisingly, in the lives of the saints. Despite the many differences of age, culture, social status, we find in the lives of the saints one common thread: each one became the person God intended him or her to be. St. John Bosco educated and cared for the youth, while St. Benedict become a hermit, and then the founder of monastic life. St. Teresa of Calcutta served the poorest of the poor in India, while St. Thérèse of Lisieux lived a hidden life of silence, solitude, and penance in a Carmelite monastery. Because they were authentic, God's light was able to shine uniquely through each one, revealing to the world in greater color the brightness of God's glory.

Imitating the saints does not mean adopting their way of speaking, thinking, or even praying. Nor does it mean going back in history to the time in which they lived in the hopes of walking in the same footsteps of the saint we admire. Imitating the saints is something much more profound. It means being inspired and enlivened by the way a particular saint has lived his or her life and using those qualities in our own life to follow Jesus more closely.

When I first discovered St. Francis of Assisi as a teenager, I knew he was the saint for me. Like him, I was restless and eager to experience more from life, yet it wasn't until my eyes were opened to the beauty of the gospel that I realized Jesus was the "more" I was desiring. Never doing anything in half measures, I, like St. Francis, threw myself into prayer, work with the poor, preaching, and anything else that could further my relationship with Christ. Like St. Francis I wanted to live a deeply contemplative life, yet I also wanted to live and work among the poor. When I discovered the Franciscan way of life, a sense of relief overwhelmed me, because I realized that what I desired and felt attracted to already existed. I didn't have to create something new.

What attracted me to St. Francis was the spirit in which he responded to the gospel. But I also know that I am not St. Francis, and I cannot and should not imitate all aspects of his personality and temperament. What the Church and the world needs from Franciscans is not another St. Francis, but men and women who, following the path of St. Francis, respond to the promptings of the Holy Spirit in their own humanity.

The ultimate question each one of us needs to ask is, What does Jesus Christ look like in me? Obviously, the answer to that question is going to look different in each person. Whether you are a doctor, a sales clerk, or a student is, in many respects, irrelevant. Being authentic means becoming the person God is calling you to be, not what he called someone else to be. God already has a Francis, a Benedict, and a Teresa. Now he's waiting for each one of us.

15
FACING DEATH

Last year on All Souls Day I was struck by these words in a sermon: "How you live is how you die." I suddenly realized the best antidote for overcoming the fear of death is a life well lived. Little did I know, I was being prepared to experience the truth of those words firsthand.

One of my teachers and friends, Fr. Andrew Apostoli, died on December 13, 2017, after losing a painful fight with cancer. When I heard that Fr. Andrew was dying, the first thing I thought was, "I want to be there." Somewhat surprised, I paused for a moment to reconsider. "Yes," I said to myself, "I need to be there."

Fr. Andrew Apostoli is known to the world as an author, retreat master, spiritual director, and teacher. To me Fr. Andrew is all those things, but more importantly, he is a humble, prayerful, and joyful Franciscan priest. I am not one of his adoring fans who have read all his books and watched all his programs. Nor would I even be considered a close friend. I am simply one of his brothers, who had the privilege of living with him for four years while I was studying for the priesthood.

After a long day of classes at the seminary, I would see Fr. Andrew arrive in chapel for Holy Hour and think, *Now here is a man who lives what I am studying.* Always lowly and unassuming, he dipped his hand in the holy water font and made a reverent sign of the cross. As he entered the chapel he genuflected for a few seconds, head down and lips uttering some words of adoration, before taking his seat in the back of the chapel.

He often called Holy Hour his "Hour of Power." Since that time before Jesus in the Eucharist was so special, he would often stand because he didn't want to fall asleep and "miss" an intimate moment. When I looked back, I might also see him leaning against the wall, head down, rosary glued to his fingers, while fighting to stay awake. He was tired of course because he had spent the whole day, and often late into the night, ministering to others while always ignoring his own personal needs.

In mid-November the doctors told us that Fr. Andrew had stage-four cancer and his life expectancy was three months. Once he received this diagnosis he moved out of the nursing home in the Bronx run by the Little Sisters of the Poor and came back to spend his last weeks at St. Leopold Friary in Yonkers, where he lived.

I was asked, along with many other friars, to take turns spending twenty-four-hour shifts with Fr. Andrew. The reason for this is simple: Death is the ultimate dark night. No matter how much faith one has, how much one has prayed, or how much theology one has studied, dying, especially with something as cruel as cancer, can be a horrifying experience of utter darkness. Nobody, even the holiest among us, is exempt from such trials.

Although each one of us dies alone, having somebody with you to attend to your physical needs and pray with you is a tremendous gift. It was the least I could do, I thought, for a man who, before he preached, lived every word that he spoke. Perhaps this is why I felt like I needed to be there: it was my way of saying thank you to a man who, though different from me in many ways, lived so beautifully.

When I was on duty with Fr. Andrew the responsibilities were twofold. First, there were his personal needs. He needed help with everything from food, clothes, to sleeping. Second, and more importantly, were his emotional and spiritual needs. Often he would wake up in the middle of the night and be confused or anxious about where he was or what he needed to do that day. I would just sit with him in his room and remind him where he was and console him with the fact that he was not late for anything.

One afternoon after praying the rosary Fr. Andrew looked at me serenely and said, "Father, I think I'm dying; can you give me last rites?" I called a few of the brothers to join me, said the prayers, and anointed him. With a look of relief, he took my hands and kissed them, reverencing not me, of course, but Jesus the High Priest whom Fr. Andrew loved his whole life.

16
THE WORK OF GOD

I never tire of hearing a person's testimony. When I listen to people speak about how they encountered God—in a near-death experience, a drug addiction, or even time in prison—I am reminded of how passionate God is in pursing us without any restrictions. Even if the testimony is relatively calm and seemingly uneventful, I am reminded of how softly God is whispering to us through the events of our life. Despite the differences in details, every testimony bears witness to a fundamental truth: we are in need of God's revelation.

In my ministry of spiritual direction the first question I always ask a new directee is, "What happened to you?" What I am essentially asking them is, "What has God done in your life that has created in you this desire for spiritual direction?" The reason I ask this question is simple: we could not have taken this step if God was not first inspiring us to move in a particular direction. In other words, our desire for spiritual direction, a vocation, or simply the desire for holiness is not ours. We are merely responding to God's work in us.

When I was in college, I was fortunate to have an academic advisor who appeared more interested in my future than I was. At the beginning of every semester, we would meet in his office for what felt more like a pep rally than an academic discussion. "Okay," he would say to me, as his eyes widened. "This semester you need to take more journalism classes than creative writing. . . .

Here is a list of possible internships you should apply for. . . . Have you considered accepting the job of editor in chief of the college newspaper like I recommended?" The more excited he became and the more suggestions he made, the more overwhelmed I began to feel. Noticing the sudden change in my disposition, he attempted to encourage me by reinforcing his motives. "I wouldn't be pushing you if I didn't think your writing had potential," he said, as he smiled and patted me on the shoulder.

Five years prior, I would have done anything to have someone excited and enthused about my writing like my academic advisor was. It was writing, I believe, that helped me navigate through those difficult and turbulent years of adolescence. Through writing I was discovering, not only who I was, but also where my place was in the world. When the time arrived to consider a career path, writing seemed like a natural fit. However, in my early years of college, something was beginning to change, or rather, I was beginning to change.

During my junior year, I scheduled an appointment with my academic advisor to inform him about a different path that God was revealing to me. As I entered his office, Dr. Baker was his usual excited and enthusiastic self.

"I was thinking," he said with a huge smile. "You need to start trying to get some of your essays published. Graduation is less than two years away, and it would be great to have some published writing to put on your résumé."

"Dr. Baker," I interrupted, "I think I'm going to be a Franciscan . . . and a priest."

He sat down, removed his glasses, and stared at me with a confused look on this face.

After a few moments of silence, he finally responded, "A what?"

"I feel like God is calling me to work with the poor and live as a Franciscan priest," I said, afraid to look him in the eye. "Maybe one day I will be a writer, but right now I believe I have to respond to God's call first."

He put his glasses on and sat back in his chair.

"I don't know what to say," he said. "I'm shocked." Another long pause. "I think you are making a great mistake. You are wasting your mind and your talent as a writer." And then he said it: "I'm really disappointed in you."

His words stung me. The one person who believed in me was telling me I was wasting my life and was disappointed in me. I left his office feeling depressed and confused and spent the next few hours walking around town wondering if he was right. As I returned to my apartment that night, I spent an hour in prayer kneeling before a crucifix, desperately begging God for light. Even though I didn't hear any voices or have any visions, I finished that time of prayer confident that this "career change" must be from God, because I could not have chosen this myself.

I then spent my senior year living more like a monk than a college student. Despite a full academic schedule, I attended daily Mass, spent an hour in prayer each day, and began fasting once a week. My free time was devoted entirely to pursuing my vocation as a Franciscan. Occasionally, a tint of sadness would envelop me as I thought about the writing, and the passion for it, that I was leaving behind. However, with each passing day, the wonder and surprise that ensued from following Jesus left me confident that I was doing God's will.

❉ ❉ ❉

Just a few months ago, I was having lunch with my best friend from college. David, though not overly religious, was a loyal and faithful friend who watched these changes occur in me firsthand. He was telling me about a conversation he had had with a few of our old friends and how when my name came up one of them kept saying, "I still don't understand what happened to him. We all thought he was going to be a writer!" Laughing, David said, "God is what happened to him." Confused by David's response, my friends asked what he meant. "Look," David replied, "we all know how much he loved writing. The only logical explanation is that something more powerful came into his life."

A big smile covered my face. "You're right," I said to David. "Thank you for understanding."

It has been almost twenty years since I told Dr. Baker that I was pursuing a vocation to religious life and priesthood. During my last year of college, Dr. Baker and I maintained a very formal relationship, and since graduation I haven't seen or heard from him. Looking back, I can understand his disappointment. He had a vision, a hope, and a plan for my life that, from a natural perspective, was one I believed would make me happy and leave me feeling fulfilled. However, when God intervened and revealed a different path, despite the initial confusion and shock it left, I knew this inspiration was not from me.

Fortunately, God does not always follow the plans and ideas we make for our lives. The real question each one of us needs to ask is, How open am I to the will of God, not only when it conforms to my desires and dreams, but especially when God's will appears different from what I first expected? By opening ourselves to God's will, we allow God to take us beyond ourselves into something much deeper than we could have imagined. In my experience, saying yes to God, even when you don't know where it will lead, can be the most beautiful and liberating experience of life.

17
THE WOMAN
KNITTING IN THE CHAPEL

Many years ago, I spent a week of retreat at Our Lady of Genesee Abbey in Upstate New York. On the last day, I returned from the monastery church after Mass to the retreat house and decided to spend a few minutes in the chapel before lunch.

As I entered and knelt in the back, I realized there was a woman sitting about five feet away from the tabernacle. As our eyes met, we exchanged a friendly smile. A few seconds later, I looked up again because I noticed something that appeared strange. She was knitting a sweater.

A few minutes later, I left the chapel and went to the dining room for lunch. Rather than enjoy the food I was eating, I spent the entire time convincing myself not only how strange it was that this woman was knitting in the chapel, but that it was wrong. A chapel, I told myself, is a place of prayer, and what this woman was doing was clearly not prayer.

On one level, perhaps I was right. A chapel, especially one that reserved the Blessed Sacrament, is a place set apart. It is not a dining hall, a workroom, or a place to socialize. When we enter a chapel, we should remember God's words to Moses: "Put off the shoes from your feet, for the place on which you are standing is holy ground" (Exodus 3:5). But I was missing something essential.

I went outside to admire the beautiful grounds of the monastery. There, in the midst of deep silence, I heard the Holy Spirit speak these words to me—*"If you loved me the way that woman does, you would not hesitate to knit in front of me."*

I had come to that day with a preconceived idea about what prayer is and what it should look like. Prayer, I believed, was essentially an activity. One was saying prayers, reading a spiritual book, or meditating on some spiritual truth. What all these activities had in common is that they were all "otherworldly." Our daily life, and our thoughts and feelings, I believed, were not important to God.

In my own zeal for holiness, I had succumbed to the most common temptation: the belief that a spiritual life was somehow separate from ordinary life. For this woman, there was no dichotomy between them. They were one and the same.

We often assume that our ordinary life is somehow not good enough or not "spiritual" enough for God. With this attitude, we end up ignoring our lives, in search of some other that contains all the necessary ingredients we believe will make us holy. For example, I have met laypeople who attempt to live like religious, much to the detriment of their families and their own vocations. In a similar fashion, I have met priests and religious who, hoping to live a more "ordinary" life, attempt to live like laypeople, thereby missing the grace being given to them in their own vocation.

The woman I saw knitting in the chapel revealed to me a deeper dimension of prayer I had not yet realized. Prayer is not just an activity directed toward "another world," but is also a way of being before God, in this world, with the life he has given me. As she sat before the Lord knitting her sweater, I imagined she spoke to him about everything in her heart. Since she was not afraid to bring knitting into her prayer, I assumed she talked to God regularly, probably when she was driving, cooking, exercising, at work, or while caring for her family.

Despite our best efforts to compartmentalize our life into various categories, there is no such thing as a spiritual life, a home life, a work life. There is just this one life to live. When we are able to view it as a whole, an ordinary task like knitting can become a means to union with God. This means there are really no distractions, just a thousand opportunities to live in the presence of God.

18
LEARNING TO PRAY

I realized, quite early on, that my vocation to religious life and priesthood was beyond me. Naturally, I was shy and quiet and questioned how I could engage in a life of public activity that included things like speaking to and directing other people. Intellectually, I was more poetic than practical and wondered how I could help people, not with their poetry, but with their lives. If my vocation was to bear fruit, I reasoned, I needed to remain open and receptive before God. In other words, if I was going to be a Franciscan and a priest, I first needed to be a man of prayer.

Prayer, like my vocation, is also beyond me. I don't know how to pray, just like I don't know how to be a Franciscan and a priest. A few years ago a deep sense of peace overwhelmed me when I arrived at the startling conclusion that prayer, like my vocation, is not something I have to figure out or master. It is already something that is happening within me. What I have to do is participate in it.

St. Paul says, "The Spirit helps us in our weakness; for we do not know how to pray as we ought, but the Spirit himself intercedes for us with sighs too deep for words" (Romans 8:26). Since prayer then is not mainly something I do, but something that is occurring within me, my primary disposition in prayer needs to be one of surrender. Hence, in prayer I try to surrender to God's presence and action within me. To help facilitate this surrender, I focus on what I like to call the "three Ls" of prayer.

First, prayer involves *looking* at God. If we are honest, most of our life is spent looking inward, not contemplating God's indwelling presence, but contemplating ourselves. To be a disciple, Jesus reminds us, we must deny ourselves and follow him (see Luke 9:23). To follow him, we must look beyond ourselves. This includes looking beyond not only our physical life but also our ideas, plans, and agenda. In prayer we escape from the narrowness and rigidity of a self-centered world and allow God to reorient us to a world more vast and beautiful than anything we could create.

Our looking in prayer might begin by gazing on a crucifix, an icon, or a scene from nature, until the One whose presence those images reveal captures our attention. As our looking becomes less self-focused, the presence of God magnifies in our lives, transforming our fear and anxiety into peace and joy.

Second, prayer involves *listening* to God. Ironic as it might sound, God is always speaking, yet he rarely uses words to communicate. Many spiritual writers have suggested that silence is God's first language. This silence, of course, is not mere emptiness or absence, but a presence much deeper than words can express. Listening to God, then, requires a certain amount of silence in prayer, so as to attune our ears to him who is beyond words.

Since listening is difficult for most of us, the Church has always recommended various aids to opening not only our ears but ultimately our hearts to this God who is always speaking. Listening to God's word in Scripture, pondering a theological teaching, or examining the movements of God in one's own life are just a few ways to help us quiet our hearts to enable us to be more attentive to God's presence.

Third, prayer involves *loving* God. Among all that has been written about God throughout history, the most probing insight into the nature of God is found by St. John when he writes, "God is love" (1 John 4:8). A hallmark of every true lover is that they desire not just gifts, praise, and acknowledgment from their beloved, but the beloved himself. As strange as this might sound, God desires us more than anything else.

The gift of ourselves to God in prayer by looking at him and listening to him allows us to love God more deeply. What we see and hear in prayer is not an angry or distant God, but a God who is patient and near. This creates in us a greater desire to love God, not merely during our times of prayer, but throughout the day. The more purely we love God, the more easily we do his will. This cannot occur, of course, without a life of prayer, since it is in prayer where we find the inspiration and the strength to love God more each day.

So prayer, as I have come to understand it, involves *looking, listening,* and *loving.* I've found on those days when prayer is most difficult that a mere look toward God, or a simple listening to him in Scripture, not only rekindles my love for God but also awakens within me a stronger sense of his presence.

We will never fully understand prayer, and we often feel like we do not pray well, but one thing is certain: without prayer, life will overwhelm us. Only by looking at God, listening to him, and loving him am I able to become the Franciscan, priest, and person God has called me to be. This begins with the simple request that will not go unanswered: "Lord, teach us to pray" (Luke 11:1).

19
LETTING GO

As a child, I often pretended my backyard was a baseball stadium. There, despite the proximity of neighbors, I would yell, dive, grunt, and cheer to various scenarios I was imagining. As time for dinner would draw near, my mom would open the window from the kitchen and ask me how much longer I would be. "Almost done, Mom," I would say. "It's the bottom of the ninth, and there are two outs." Then, as the thousands of fans were standing and cheering in anticipation of the final out, I struck out the last batter to win the game, as my teammates rushed the mound and carried me off on their shoulders.

Somewhere, probably around the age of thirteen, I became self-conscious and started to wonder, *What do my neighbors think about me yelling and cheering in my backyard? What are other people going to think of me if they see me? Is this how a thirteen-year-old is supposed to act?* These were sobering thoughts. I realized what I was doing was not wrong, but that life was calling me forward, and if I wanted to move forward, I needed to let go of where I was and accept where life was taking me.

If someone were to ask, "What is the secret of life?" I would answer, "Letting go."

This phrase, unfortunately, is often misunderstood and misused. It can sound at times cold and even harsh. I have heard people use this phrase as a means to justify their selfishness.

"I am letting go of this situation," one might say, when what is really happening is that they are refusing an opportunity that requires generosity and self-gift. I've also heard the phrase used with a deep sense of resignation and loss of hope. Then it seems to mean, "I give up."

What I mean by letting go is not self-preservation or giving up, but acceptance of life as it really is.

Each of us possesses an image of what we think life should look like. When that image is frustrated we think there is something wrong with life. We blame God, other people, and circumstances for the reason our image of life has been thwarted. Perhaps the real problem is not life, but our expectation of the way it should be.

As a spiritual director, I have often accompanied people throughout a discernment process and continue meeting with them as they begin their vocation. After three months of living their vocation I ask them how they are doing. The response is generally similar: "The community, my spouse, the ministry, my work, [fill in the blank] is great. I couldn't imagine things to be any better." As the months go by, the conversation changes dramatically. Generally, things remain good, but the community, spouse, ministry, or work is no longer the perfect supplement to their life. They discover, much to their surprise, that their vocation looks nothing like they once imagined it would.

At this point a natural question arises, *Did I discern properly?* The majority of the time the person *has* discerned properly. They are now being invited to let go of those former images about how life is supposed to look, and embrace the life God is giving them. This invitation from God, though frightening at first, is exactly the food our hearts crave. By abandoning ourselves completely to God beyond what we can see and understand, we begin to experience that our life, though not perfect, contains exactly what we need to grow in faith, hope, and love.

Perhaps this is the greatest test we Christians face. We often assume that because we are following Jesus our lives will look and be a certain way.

Once when the disciples were arguing about who was the greatest, Jesus informed them, "He who is least among you all is the one who is great" (Luke 9:48). This was not the answer any of them expected or desired; yet if they were going to keep following Jesus, they had to let go of what they thought that should look like.

We begin by pursuing the life we want for ourselves, but end up living the life God wants for us. After the Resurrection, Jesus says to Peter, "Truly, truly, I say to you, when you were young, you girded yourself and walked where you would; but when you are old, you will stretch out your hands, and another will gird you and carry you where you do not wish to go" (John 21:18). It is only by letting go, with childlike trust, that we allow God to lead us beyond anything we could have imagined.

20
EMBARRASSMENTS

Shortly after I was ordained a priest, a friend asked me what my experience was like thus far. Somewhat hesitantly I said, "Embarrassing." He began to laugh. Assuming I was joking, he asked me again. "No, seriously, what is it like to be a priest?" "Embarrassing," I replied again, this time without hesitation.

I always knew I was called to be a priest. The most peaceful moments of my childhood were when I was serving Mass as an altar boy. Though I was too young to understand what was happening, my heart encountered this profound joy each time I served Mass. The candles, incense, and paintings were signs pointing me beyond this world. Though my childhood was blessed, I began yearning for this other world that I experienced each day at Mass.

The priest, I began to realize, had a pivotal role in this experience. He was not a coach, a sergeant, or a stage director, but simply a man chosen by God to facilitate this transcendent experience. Whether he was celebrating Mass, hearing confessions, or giving last rites to the dying, the priest brought heaven with him through his priestly ministry. The day I realized this I remember asking myself, *What else could I want from life?*

What I found perhaps to be most remarkable was that the priests, at least the ones I met as a kid, were not the holiest, smartest, or best speakers I encountered. There was nothing that distinguished them from others in outward appearances. They were, like everyone, frail and broken, struggling with their humanity, while trying to reconcile how God could call somebody like them to this vocation.

In my second year of priesthood I had the honor of baptizing my brother-in-law during the Easter Vigil. He was raised without any faith, and after several years of marriage to my sister he decided he wanted to become Catholic. After I poured water over him three times, baptizing him "in the name of the Father and the Son and the Holy Spirit," I saw something on him I had never witnessed before: a smile that radiated pure joy. Struck by the simple beauty of the moment I embraced him and said, "Welcome home."

Perhaps my greatest joy as a priest is hearing confessions. Over the years I have heard countless confessions and have witnessed the immediate change inside a person once the words of absolution are spoken. Often people come to confession burdened, anxious, and afraid, yet they always leave confession with the hope that is born from experiencing the mercy of God. Once an elderly man, old enough to be my grandfather, kissed my hands after confession and said, "Thank you, Father. You have given me my life back." Immediately, tears flowed from my eyes and I was reduced to silence.

Finally, there is the Eucharist. Whether it is a friary chapel, a cathedral, or a simple country church, heaven enters this world through my hands under the appearance of bread and wine. In my first few weeks as a priest my hands would begin to shake during the consecration and I would ask myself after each Mass, "Did that really just happen?" In the midst of this confusion a fellow Franciscan said to me one morning after Mass, "Thank you, Father, for the Eucharist." I was completely dumbstruck. Later in the day I realized that without the priest, there is no Eucharist. Once more, the tears flowed and I was again reduced to silence.

In all these events, I am not a mere observer. I am, and I say this with deep humility, the bridge on which God travels to meet his people. The priest is, obviously, not the only way for this encounter to occur, but he remains a consistent and definite means of God's presence in this world.

When I told my friend that being a priest was embarrassing, what I most of all meant was that it is humbling. I am somewhat shy, never comfortable in large crowds, and certainly never comfortable being any sort of leader. I was just an average student in school. I did far more daydreaming than studying. Like the prophet Jeremiah I tried to tell God, "I do not know how to speak, for I am only a youth" (Jeremiah 1:6). Regardless of what I perceived as apparent obstacles, God felt differently.

Seven years have passed since my friend asked me what it is like being a priest. If I were asked that question today, I would probably respond once again by saying, "Embarrassing," but this time I would be sure to add how grateful and joyful I have become for all the embarrassment it's caused me.

21
SUFFERING REVISITED

When I entered religious life as a twenty-three-year-old, I was passionate, idealistic, and determined. I said goodbye to the world without blinking an eye and threw myself wholeheartedly into my vocation. I devoured the teachings and perfectly obeyed all the rules of my community and the Church. Though it wasn't my primary motivation, a part of me thought if I just did what was right and believed what was true, God would protect me from suffering. After all, isn't this the promise God makes through the psalmist?

> Because you have made the LORD your refuge,
> the Most High your habitation,
> no evil shall befall you,
> no scourge come near your tent. (Psalm 91:9–10)

Within the first two years of my religious vocation, life unleashed a series of events that led me to a crisis of faith. One of my best friends from college, a devout and beautiful woman named Nicole, was diagnosed with cancer at age twenty-three. Six months later, filled with shock and sorrow, I was reunited with all of our friends from college at her funeral, as we asked God why.

My mother, who was already ill then, was slipping deeper and deeper into Alzheimer's and depression. As the days drew on, she lost the desire to live, wanting only to be reunited with her parents, whom she so desperately missed, despite having a family of her own who needed her. Although I told myself that God was all that I needed, I was still, in many respects, a little boy who needed a mother to console him.

Living in a religious community, I not only experienced "how good and pleasant it is when brothers live in unity" (Psalm 133:1), but I also encountered the misunderstandings, annoyances, and tensions that are part of that unity. Despite the many hours of prayer, the grace of the sacraments, and strong fraternal support, nonetheless forgiveness, charity, and generosity were not getting any easier. In fact, in some ways, they were becoming more difficult.

I examined myself repeatedly and thought, *I must be doing something wrong. Perhaps I need to fast more, pray more, or make another general confession.* I sought counsel from books and spiritual directors, believing there must be a solution to my problems. Once I found it, I thought, these trials would cease.

After much searching, I began to ask, "Is this what life with God looks like?"

Suddenly, one day with this question echoing in my heart, I heard a voice that said, "Yes, this is exactly what life with God looks like." Then came the real stinger: "Do you think that you are exempt from human suffering because of your vocation to religious life?"

Even though Jesus had clearly said, "If any man would come after me, let him deny himself and take up his cross daily and follow me" (Luke 9:23), part of me believed that those words did not apply in my situation.

Without realizing it, I had reduced Jesus to the equivalent of an antibiotic. If I just follow the prescription of prayer, fasting, and obedience, then all of this suffering would disappear and I would return again to good health. Without question, Jesus is our refuge and our physician, but he protects us and heals us in a way much different than our limited minds can comprehend.

Looking back at those first two years of religious life, I realized that the suffering I encountered during that time was therapeutic for my soul, and led me to an intimacy with God I hadn't yet encountered. In those moments of suffering, and all the many ones that have occurred since, I am reminded of an important truth: God is bigger than this world. Without diminishing the importance of our earthly lives, our destiny lies beyond the limits of this world. "For here we have no lasting city" (Hebrews 13:14).

Despite our best efforts to avoid suffering, no one is exempt. We too often think suffering is a sign that one has done something wrong, or that if we just try harder, it will go away. Many people who have just experienced a conversion, or begin the initial stages of a vocation, assume this is true. I realized how this picture is incomplete. By using God simply to avoid trials I was living only for myself. Suffering, oddly enough, has enabled me to live for God.

THE OTHER
WHO LOVES US

Every day we stand before an unsolvable problem: life. The people we encounter, the events that occur, and the places we are led often leave us frustrated and confused. If we are honest, most of the time we don't understand why things happen the way they do. This can lead some to conclude that we're all alone, that life is only a series of random events with no rhyme or reason.

Faith views things differently. Without denying the puzzling nature of life, faith attests that beyond the darkness, beyond the veil of this world, there is an "Other," who not only guides the universe but also guides each one of us. This Other not only guides our lives but also loves us in a way we cannot comprehend.

I was reminded of this truth during an unexpected conversation in an unusual setting. I had just finished giving a retreat in Dallas and was on my way to Los Angeles for another retreat. As I boarded the plane and sat down, I began to consider how I should spend these next four hours. Typically, flying provides an ideal opportunity to write, because of the minimal amount of interruptions available.

I opened my computer and began reading my latest reflection. The flight attendants announced that the gates would be closing soon and we should prepare for takeoff. I looked around and noticed that the plane was entirely full, except for the seat next to me. Suddenly, a woman who appeared to be in her late forties with black dyed hair, ripped blue jeans, and sunglasses boarded the plane.

"I didn't think I would make it," she said to the flight attendant, as she tried to catch her breath.

"Just in time," she said. "Have a seat. We will be taking off shortly."

As she sat down next to me, she placed her bag under her seat, pulled out her phone, and began fixing her hair. While she buckled her seatbelt, we smiled at each other and I said hello.

"Oh wow," she said. "Are you like a monk?"

Laughing, I said, "Well, sort of. Technically I'm a friar, a Franciscan and a priest."

"I'm a Jewish agnostic," she said. "My ex-husband is Muslim and my brother just became a Buddhist."

I returned her wow with one of my own, and added, "Do you know any Hindus? Then we would have all five major world religions represented!"

We both laughed as the plane began to make its way down the runway. Then, as we began to takeoff, she looked at me nervously and asked, "Would you mind talking?"

"Of course not," I said with a smile. "What would you like to talk about?"

"Well, my name is Joan." And so it began.

For the next three hours, Joan did most of the talking. She was raised in a Jewish home, where faith was more cultural than personal. Her father was always working, leaving her home alone with a mother who was always telling Joan everything that was wrong with her. Desperate for the affection of a father, she began a series of relationships with older men, each worse than the previous. Desiring love and acceptance more than an education or a career, she dropped out of college at twenty.

Wanting to escape her past, she left Brooklyn and moved to San Francisco to begin a new life. After drifting from one job to the next, she finally met a man, whom she described as a "dream come true," while working as a bartender in the Bay Area. Alan, a few years older than Joan, was a successful businessman who appeared to have his life together. He was young, rich, and attractive, and most importantly, interested in Joan. The two began dating and got married six months later.

Three years into their marriage a secret from Alan's past came back to haunt him: a drug addiction that Alan believed he'd conquered came back into his life, and Alan began using again. With two small children at home and a husband who was using drugs, Joan turned to alcohol for consolation. Soon their marriage was on the verge of collapsing. Nine months later they got divorced.

When I met Joan on the plane she had just finished a month-long rehab program. She was eager to see her two boys again, who had stayed with her sister. As she showed me several pictures of them on her phone, tears came pouring out of her eyes. "I just don't know what I'm doing," she said. "I don't know how to live. I don't know how to be a mom. I don't understand life."

She was interrupted by the flight attendant's voice over the intercom. We had just begun our descent into Los Angeles, and we would be landing in a few minutes. Joan took out a tissue from her purse and began wiping her eyes. Looking at me with a smile she said, "Thank you for listening to me."

"You're welcome," I said. "Thank you for sharing all of that. It takes courage to be that vulnerable."

"Well," she said, "if I can't trust a monk, whom can I trust?" We both laughed.

"Do you mind if I say something, Joan?" I asked.

"No, not at all," she said. "You think I'm crazy, right?"

"Don't be silly. You're not any crazier than I am!" I said. "You mentioned that you don't know what you are doing, that you don't know how to live, and that you don't know how to be a mom."

Nodding, she said, "It's true."

"Perhaps you don't have to know," I said. "Look, here we are at thirty thousand feet. How did you get here after all that you have been through? It wasn't your family who got you here. It wasn't your husband, or even you. It seems to me that there is somebody else, an Other, who has been carrying you and has got you here to this point."

"You mean God?" she said.

"Yes."

"Every time I hear the word *God* I think of my mother telling me how pretty all the other young girls were at synagogue and how she wished I would spend more time on my appearance so I could look like them."

I closed my eyes out of sadness. "I'm so sorry that was your experience," I said.

We were both silent for a few moments. "Perhaps the best place to start," I said, "is with the realization that there must be an Other who cares for you, loves you, and is guiding you in your life. If not, then how you are here? How am I here?"

There was a long pause. She looked out the window and I could see in the reflection the hint of a smile on her face.

"This Other," I continued, "is not an idea or some sort of energy out in the universe. He is personal, forgiving, and is not obsessed with your past. He is love, and without him we couldn't get out of bed in the morning. Life is impossible without an awareness of the love that sustains us. If we want to understand our life, then the most sane thing we can do is open ourselves to this Other as best we can, and he will take care of the rest."

By this point our plane had landed and we were taxing to our gate. We remained in silence for those few moments until the flight attendants announced we could unbuckle our seatbelts and begin exiting the plane. As Joan and I grabbed our bags we walked together out of the plane and into the airport. Before we went our separate ways, she looked at me with tears in her eyes.

"I do believe there is an Other who is sustaining me," she said. "There has to be, otherwise I don't know how I would be standing today."

I smiled, "So do I, Joan."

We hugged goodbye and began to walk in separate directions. A few seconds later I heard her yell, "Hey, Father."

I turned around.

"Will you pray for me?"

I smiled at her. "Of course, I will. Please pray for me too."

"I will," she said as she put on her sunglasses and disappeared into the crowd.

BREATHING

On average, a person takes 16 breaths a minute, 960 breaths an hour, and 23,040 breaths a day. Like most people, I have spent my life oblivious to this ordinary human act, until recently.

I was sitting in my backyard reading a book and closed my eyes for a few moments of reflection. Suddenly, my thoughts disappeared. The ideas I was meditating on had reached their limit. Out of that silence I felt my chest expand as I inhaled fresh air. I calmly listened as I exhaled and continued to watch, in almost childlike wonder, the sound of each inhale and exhale.

I put the book down and remained sitting, paying attention to my breathing. After about twenty minutes had gone by I opened my eyes and almost didn't recognize where I was. I hadn't moved yet something was different. The pine trees I see everyday as I look out my window were still there. The neighbors' blue truck hadn't moved from their driveway, and the pond a few hundred feet away from my house was still resting in its usual place. Externally life was normal, but internally a shift had occurred. It was as if I were looking at the world around me, not with the familiar eyes that tend to gloss over each moment, but with the eyes of a child for whom everything is fresh and exciting.

What amazed me was not that I was breathing, but that I had never paid attention to it before. How many of us have lived many years and never reflected on this ordinary human act? Yet what I found most ironic about this experience was that paying attention to my breathing was not simply a physiological or psychological experience of myself. It was an experience of God, who felt closer to me than my own body. It was as if God were breathing inside of me.

Many of the world's religions speak of paying attention to one's breath as a valuable spiritual practice. It is used, not as a tool to escape reality, but as a way to transcend the endless dialogue that occurs in our overactive minds. Once we can move beyond that chatter, many religions say, we see things in a purer light. The rationale for this is simple: breathing helps us to transcend an overly rationalistic outlook that, through it can be helpful in thinking about God, can often become a block in experiencing God more deeply. One stands, then, from this perspective, before reality not as a teacher but as a student. It is this posture that allows one a more genuine experience of the Ultimate Reality that we call God.

Christians can be uncomfortable or suspicious speaking about the spirituality of breathing because they associate it with Eastern meditation practices. But breathing has been an essential part of our faith from the beginning. The book of Genesis tells us that "the Lord God formed man of dust from the ground, and *breathed* into his nostrils the breath of life; and man became a living being" (Genesis 2:7). On Easter night, after Jesus "re-created" the world by his passion, death, and resurrection, he met his fearful disciples and "*breathed* on them, and said to them, 'Receive the Holy Spirit'" (John 20:22). It is the breath of God that gives us life, both physically and spiritually. Every breath we take, then, is a reminder not only of our dependence on God but also of our union with him.

I often find myself pulled in many directions. I am constantly juggling what I believe are three areas the Lord is calling me to: prayer, writing, and preaching. Despite these activities, there is always somebody to help, there are many communal and familial responsibilities always at hand, and then there is just life, with all its surprises and annoyances. I spend most of my day without a sensible or consoling experience of God's presence. In other words, I stumble around from one moment to the next, attempting to walk more "by faith, not by sight" (2 Corinthians 5:7). Despite my best efforts, I often find myself bumping into everything around me because, in reality, I walk more by sight than by faith. Though I believe in God and know he is present to me, providing me with every grace I am in need of, I often do not feel this in any tangible or sensible way.

Stopping, if only for a few moments, and becoming aware of my breathing has provided me an opportunity to ground myself in reality.

On days when I try to control life, this truth can be utterly terrifying because it reveals my own poverty and need, something all of us, including myself, would rather talk about than experience. On days when trust is greater and the desire to surrender myself to God permeates my heart, this truth is liberating because it enables me to place my hope where it belongs: outside of myself and onto God.

Paying attention to one's breathing, I have realized, can also be a way of prayer. If the simple act of breathing can remind us of the reality of God, that same breath can also be a means of surrender to God. Through my breathing, I am saying yes to life, not as I want it, but as it really is. This yes to our life is essentially a yes to God, since "the breath of the Almighty gives me life" (Job 33:4).

24
A DIFFERENT JOURNEY

I remember awakening each morning to the sound of nature. Birds were singing in unison throughout the valley, while squirrels, scurrying through leaves and sticks, chased each other up and down trees. Each morning, elk would visit the river located about five hundred feet from our campsite, while eagles glided overhead.

I was surrounded as far as I could see by enormous snowcapped mountains. Trees, rivers, and giant boulders filled the countryside. There was not a trace of civilization anywhere. At times, I had to pinch myself to make sure this wasn't a dream. It was, without a doubt, the most spectacular scenery I had ever witnessed.

We began each day promptly at seven in the morning. The day's activities included mountain biking, hiking, fishing, rafting, and swimming. If we were lucky, and our guide had the proper equipment, he would take us rock climbing for a few hours in the late afternoon. Finally, as the sun was beginning to set, we returned to our camp exhausted, only to find a feast prepared over an open fire waiting for us.

A few months earlier, some friends, realizing I needed a break from the city, graciously paid for me to spend a week with them on vacation in Colorado. "It would be rejuvenating," my friend Mike said, "and refreshing. Besides, I can't imagine a more beautiful place to spend a week of vacation." He was right. It was the perfect scenario in the perfect location, and yet I was miserable.

I always love spending time outdoors and have spent many hours mountain biking and swimming, but there was something different about this. The difference, I discovered, was me. As a teenager, I would go hiking and camping in the woods because I was naturally attracted to the quiet beauty of nature. Yet on a deeper level, I went to the woods in search of its source. Nature, for me, was a sign pointing beyond itself. Rather than stop at the sign, my entire being yearned for that Reality to which the sign was pointing. If I followed the sign frequently, I reasoned, I would eventually go beyond it.

Once I consciously made the decision to follow Jesus and returned wholeheartedly to the Church, my focus shifted from a purely exterior journey to the discovery of an interior one. Although I continued to visit beautiful sites and had fun with friends, I began to spend more time alone in my room, a church, or some other quiet place where I could read, pray, and spend time in silence. Suddenly, without going anywhere, I was traveling to much deeper places than I ever thought imaginable.

When I began this vacation in Colorado I had been a Franciscan for twelve years and a priest for three. I was accustomed to several hours of prayer and silence each day. My friends, who had only good intentions, believed I would have more fun if I did more activities. The problem was, then, that I found myself with no time, and ironically, no space, for prayer. Every morning I celebrated Mass and had about ten minutes of prayer afterward before the events of the day began.

By late morning, after already hiking and swimming for several hours, all I desired was a few moments of stillness. My heart and mind were touched deeply by the wonder that surrounded me, yet it wasn't enough. In order to truly appreciate and experience the beauty of this place, I had to move beyond its signs to its source. Without this deeper contact, the joy that was available in this moment became threatened. Unfortunately there was no time. The next event was waiting for us.

As evening arrived, I was surrounded by friends who loved me, but a deep feeling of loneliness overwhelmed me. At camp, my friends sang songs, told jokes, and recounted childhood memories. I appreciated their presence and enjoyed listening, yet I felt a deep void in our group. Without prayer in my day, I felt alienated, not only from other people, but also from the beauty that surrounded me. "Is something wrong with me?" I asked myself. "Here I am in this beautiful place on a free vacation, and I am not happy. Am I being selfish? Am I being too religious?"

Despite my best efforts to alter my mood, I was unsuccessful. As the days progressed, my sadness only increased. The more activities we did, the worse I felt. On our last morning in Colorado, one of my friends suggested we do another long hike before going to the airport. "Please," I sighed, "I've had enough. Can we just go to the airport?"

My friends were shocked. "Is everything okay?"

"Yes . . . I'm sorry. I'm just tired and don't want to miss my flight," I said, which wasn't entirely true.

As I boarded the plane to fly home, I felt confused and frustrated. Thankfully, I had the entire row on the plane to myself. *Finally,* I thought, *space simply to be alone with God.* I stared out the window and began to speak from the depths of my heart. As I began my evening prayer I felt a deep peace within my soul. "For God alone my soul waits in silence" (Psalm 62:1). How often I'd prayed those words, but this time they held a deeper meaning for me.

I spent the rest of the flight in silence, reading Scripture, speaking to God, and just listening. While we were beginning our descent into Newark airport, I felt a wave of consolation overwhelm me.

I don't think I was being ungrateful or selfish in my responses to that amazing trip with my friends. My trouble came from my desires for a different journey, one that would take me deeper, to a place beyond this world, where my soul can find the space it needs and the rest it most of all desires.

MISTAKEN IDENTITY

I can't remember exactly how old I was, but as a young boy I asked myself an important question: "Who am I?" *After all,* I thought, *what is the point of living if you don't know who you are?* In my innocence, I assumed everyone was fascinated by this question and that most people were eager to discover the answer. Needless to say, I was thoroughly confused to realize this was not so.

Many people, I learned, live on the surface of life. They place their hope in things like social status, strength and influence, physical appearance, or wealth to reveal to them who they are. I often heard people say things like, "I am a doctor," "I am an honor student," or "I am poor," implying a person's real identity is something exterior. Ignorant of any other possibilities, it was here that began my own journey of self-discovery.

For me, childhood was consumed by baseball. Every spare moment was spent either working on my pitching in my backyard or at batting practice in some field nearby. After experiencing a tiny amount of success, I witnessed a bizarre set of associations begin to unfold: people were identifying me with baseball. I was the kid with a good arm, who helped win this game, a pitcher who was turning this team around. I began to digest every word that was spoken about this mysterious person whom everyone was identifying as "me." I was a good pitcher. I was a baseball player. I was an athlete.

As I entered my teenage years, this identity proved insufficient. My feelings, emotions, and even my physical appearance were in a constant state of change. Due to these sudden and often radical changes occurring both within me and without, I became terribly insecure and afraid. It was during this time when I encountered the power of music. I would read the lyrics of different songs, particularly rock songs, and feel understood. I could relate to the singer's pain, confusion, and desire for love.

Within weeks of this discovery, I was teaching myself how to play guitar. A few months later, I was playing in a band with three other guys. Before we knew it, we were playing gigs on a regular basis and people, once again, began to talk. "I love the lyrics you write." "You are a great bass player." Enjoying the way all this sounded, I believed them. Now I was creative, artistic, and a good bass player. Now I was a musician.

By the time I entered college, baseball and music had both become distant memories. I began to explore a new world of intrigue: philosophy. I had no desire for a career, an impressive résumé, or academic honors when I began college. I was genuinely seeking wisdom, yet as more people discovered that I was a philosophy major, another strange occurrence took place: people began to label me as intelligent, wise, and even spiritual. "You are a philosopher." "You are smart." I began to wonder if maybe these people saw something about me that I didn't. Then, since I enjoyed the way these acclamations felt, I decided they were right. I was satisfied to be all of the good things that people said of me.

To say that I was desperate to find out who I was would be an understatement. The question gnawed at me continually, and I looked for the answer in all the wrong places.

As good as all these things are, I never was, nor will be, a baseball player, musician, or philosopher. Likewise, people are never the sum of their careers, social status, influence, or health. Our identity always transcends the categories of this world. "You are no longer strangers and sojourners, but you are fellow citizens with the saints and members of the household of God" (Ephesians 2:19). Even more simply, the apostle says, "Your life is hid with Christ in God" (Colossians 3:3).

We belong to God. All the roles and functions we might play in this world cannot add to or alter the identity God has imprinted within us. I hope you find this in your life.

A wealthy man I met during a parish mission once expressed it this way: "I am a Christian, but the role I play in this world is that of a doctor."

The temptation to find our true identity among the finite things of this world is always present. Often, when children leave home parents can experience an identity crisis since there are no longer any children to care for. After fulfilling such an important role for so many years, it is easy to identify oneself with that role. "I am a parent," they might say. "What do I do now?" With no children to care for, they are forced to find a deeper answer to the question, Who am I?

Even now I am tempted to find my identity in the things of God rather than God himself. When I was a novice, a wise old priest used to say to us, "Don't inhale." He was referring to any praise and admiration we might receive from preaching or by the witness of our religious life. He was reminding us that what is said about us never paints a complete picture. The danger is that, by inhaling—believing what is said about us to be a reflection of our true identity—we run the risk of attempting to solve the mystery of our identity without all the proper pieces. The finite things of this world, good though they are, are incomplete and unable to reveal to us who we really are.

After so many failed attempts to identify myself among the things of this world, I think I am now able to recognize exactly what this always turns out to be: another case of mistaken identity.

SEEING LISA

Lisa and I met in the seventh grade. Her family had recently moved from Philadelphia into my neighborhood, and after talking each morning at the bus stop, we became close friends. As neighbors who were the same age and in the same grade, we found our lives, without any real planning on our part, becoming closely intertwined.

When Lisa's first boyfriend suddenly broke up with her in tenth grade she was devastated. We skipped school together and spent the whole day eating ice cream and playing video games. Despite being a bit upset about our skipping school, Lisa's mother called to thank me for being there for her. When Lisa was hospitalized a few weeks after our graduation from high school with a mysterious illness, I spent almost every day at the hospital with her family, just being present to her and helping her in any way I could.

When I was ordained a priest, Lisa, a non-Christian, was sitting in the front row of the cathedral hours before the ordination began, appearing more excited and enthused than many of my devout friends. It didn't matter to her that she did not understand exactly what was happening. She knew that my ordination was a major moment in my life, and that was enough for her. Two years later, when my mother died, she drove six hours from Washington, DC, to attend the funeral and spend time with my family as we grieved.

What is unusual about our friendship is that Lisa and I disagree on almost everything, from politics, to social issues, to religion. Yet after each conversation, whether it is a friendly one or a heated debate, we always affirm our love for each other. Genuine love, respect, and friendship, we believe, runs deeper than ideology. Thankfully, we have never permitted our convictions to disrespect or harm the other. If either of us would utter a harsh word in the midst of a fiery conversation, both of us, sooner or later, would apologize. Our differences have stretched us to become more patient and better listeners. We have learned, much to our own discomfort, that life is not black and white, and that each person is a work in progress.

Every person is made in the image and likeness of God (Genesis 1:26). This statement, found in the very beginning of the Bible, is a reminder that the human person cannot be reduced to merely worldly categories. Too often we identify people based entirely on their political persuasions or opinions. These aspects of an individual may be relevant, but they are never in and of themselves a portrait.

A friend of mine recently told me that his family had to cancel Thanksgiving with his relatives this year, because of what he described as "political differences" among various family members. Both families decided that they couldn't spend the holidays with each other because of how they voted in the previous election. This story is a sad commentary on our highly charged political climate. What is tragic about it is not that people believe different things, but that they have allowed those beliefs to create divisions, even among their own family.

Nothing is as important as our faith. But even when we disagree in religious or theological matters it is important that we continue to love the other person as God does.

Over the years, I have spoken to many people about their religious beliefs. At times, just the mere presence of a Catholic priest can elicit strong reactions. Most people, regardless of their experience with Catholicism, are generally respectful, even if they disagree with the tenets of the Church. However, a few times I have encountered people who have been extremely disrespectful, either by laughing at me, mocking me, or even spitting on me in public.

In these moments, I have tried, though never perfectly, to follow Jesus's command to "love your enemies and pray for those who persecute you" (Matthew 5:43). There is a part of me that wants to lash back at them, judge them, and even mock them in return; but I realize that attitude only creates more division. And if I do that, I will have failed to see the other person in his or her entirety. Instead, I try as best I can to listen, understand their viewpoint, and pray for them. Despite our differences, they, like me, are made in the image and likeness of God. As radical as this approach might appear in our current culture, this is what Jesus did throughout his public ministry.

I am not ignoring the real consequences that ideas have, but a person is not an idea. The Gospels recount how Jesus ate with Pharisees, tax collectors, and sinners, three groups that differed widely in thought and action with Jesus. Rather than seeing these people through the labels and categories in which others viewed them, Jesus saw each as having infinite value, and for whom he would give his life. Genuine discipleship requires that we at least try to do the same.

Lisa and I continue to live very different lives and believe very different things. Still, after twenty-five years of friendship, these differences have not eliminated our love for each other, nor have they lessened our mutual respect. We speak each month on the phone, and see each other about once a year, usually around the holidays, regardless of how either one of us has voted. Despite all the people who have come and gone in my life, Lisa has remained constant and, I am confident, will always be my close friend.

I would even say that Lisa has been one of my greatest teachers. She has forced me to examine my views more thoroughly and see things from a different perspective. Her presence, and the challenge that she initiates in my life, has helped me to love people more deeply. Because of her I try to see people less as the world does, and more from the viewpoint of the Cross.

UNPACKING

Every time I travel I seem to encounter a common scenario. As passengers are boarding the plane, there's always one person who believes that his bag, despite being too big, can fit in the last tiny space available in the overhead bins. While the flight attendant arrives to assess the situation, a simple look at the bag is often sufficient for them to determine whether the bag will fit.

"I'm sorry," they often say. "The bag won't fit. We can check your bag and you can pick it up at baggage when we arrive at our destination."

"No, I think I can make it fit," the passenger will respond, which is followed by a minute or two of pushing, maneuvering, and attempting to manipulate the space that simply isn't there.

"It's not going to fit," the flight attendant says again with a smile. "Let me take your bag and check it." With a look of confusion on his face, the passenger surrenders his bag to the flight attendant and sits down, looking somewhat annoyed. Unfortunately, this is not just one random passenger on a particular flight. This is the way most of us approach life. We are greatly overpacked.

Our society has convinced us that our lives are inadequate. We are told what is wrong with our bodies, families, careers, and so on. The answer, society concludes, is waiting for us "out there," whether it is in the form of a surgery, a new job, or some other thing that promises to perfect our many imperfections. Before we know it, our homes, workplaces, and, more importantly, our hearts are filled with stuff we never needed.

A similar tragedy is played out in the spiritual life. I often meet people who believe that being a good Christian comes from reading certain books, attending certain retreats, and being active in various ministries. They are shocked when they discover a fellow Christian who is not walking an identical path. "How could you have not read this book or attended this retreat?" they often ask, as if holiness were merely the result of completing a spiritual checklist. Unfortunately, these spiritual demands usually result not in transformation but burnout.

The spiritual life is not a process of acquiring things, but more a process of getting rid of things. Of course reading books, attending retreats, and becoming involved in ministry are all important and necessary components of a well-balanced Christian life. However, the purpose of these things is to awaken, not install, God's life within us. The reason for this is simple: in Christ, we already have everything we need. The problem is that we don't realize it.

St. Paul reminds us, "I give thanks to God always for you because of the grace of God which was given you in Christ Jesus, that in every way you were enriched in him with all speech and all knowledge . . . so that you are not lacking in any spiritual gift" (1 Corinthians 1:4–7). When I mention these words to individuals in spiritual direction or to a group on retreat, most people struggle to believe them. In fact, most of us believe the opposite.

When I first began preaching, the first place I would go to prepare was not the chapel, but the library. I would spend almost my entire prayer time not praying, but reading commentaries and everybody else's thoughts on the Scriptures, because I believed

I lacked the necessary gifts to preach effectively. Thankfully, this process was so exhausting that it only lasted a few weeks. Now, most if not all my preparation for homilies occurs, not by reading commentaries, but by sitting in silence before God in prayer. Once I've unpacked the clutter, I find I have more room for God.

So where do we start unpacking? The most obvious thing to start unpacking is sin. It is no coincidence that the first words we read of Jesus are "Repent, and believe in the gospel" (Mark 1:15). Why does Jesus begin here? Consider our everyday human experience: for example, if one spouse spends an entire week ignoring or speaking unkindly toward the other, their relationship is going to be strained. That behavior might not destroy the marriage, but it does damage it and creates a rift. A simple "I'm sorry" followed by love and respect can begin the healing and strengthen the relationship instead.

What is true in human relationships is also true in our relationship with God. We all at times say or think things that are contrary to what Jesus has revealed to us. If there is some sin in our lives that we are struggling with, then that is the place where this unpacking needs to begin. To facilitate the unpacking, we must cultivate friendships that promote holiness and not worldliness. We must avoid those places or situations that tempt us and can lead us astray. We must give God time each day in prayer and, through the sacrament of reconciliation, humbly confess our sins with absolute confidence in God's mercy. Through such simple means, we can begin to unpack what's been weighing us down. All this, of course, is not an overnight process, but requires patience, trust, and fidelity. Jesus himself says, "By your endurance you will gain your lives" (Luke 21:19).

Removing serious sin from our lives is only the beginning of Christian discipleship. There is still more unpacking to do. Each of us carries a certain amount of baggage that needs to be purified by God's grace. This baggage appears in many forms, whether it is through emotional and psychological wounds, painful memories we have repressed, or defense mechanisms that we have acquired to protect ourselves. Regardless of the forms it takes, the baggage we are carrying cannot fit into the life God is inviting us to.

The world, often with good intentions, wants us to believe that we are strong, competent, and capable of anything. As Christians, we believe that our strength, competency, and capability are not something we possess on our own but are ours because of Christ who lives inside of us. St. Paul says it perfectly: "I can do all things in him who strengthens me" (Philippians 4:13). To experience God's strength in our lives does not require our going anywhere or doing something extraordinary. It is simply a process of unpacking, since in our ultimate destination, heaven, no baggage is necessary. With God, we have everything we need.

BEYOND DEATH

I have lived almost my entire life in the northeastern United States. Every year a sublime mystery occurs. The leaves begin to sing. Throughout the spring and summer they have been quiet, simply blending in, and clothing the trees in simple attire. But then, in mid-October, they are approaching an encore. For the next few weeks the woods become a glorious spectacle of bright red and orange, yellow and brown. People take pictures, hiking trails fill up, and artists attempt to paint the majestic scene while it lasts.

The season of fall provides us with a mirror in which we can contemplate something much deeper than the changing of seasons—namely, the mystery of death. Throughout our lives, we will experience many deaths. These deaths will be as unique as each person. For some they could come as an illness, a financial problem, or the end of a relationship. It could be the death of a friend or parent, a dream that was shattered, or trying to move through a period of depression or loneliness. For others, it could be an unappreciative boss or a prayer that God seems to be ignoring. Death, at least according to the rhythm of nature, is not an end but is always a necessary means to something greater.

When my mother first became depressed, life as I knew it had ended. A few months earlier, when my grandmother passed away, my mother never recovered. Almost immediately my family recognized a change in her. She'd lost her joy and enthusiasm for life. Instead of engaging the family in conversation, she gazed out the window, bypassing our conversation and my need for affirmation. Most of all, my mother, who was always strong and confident in all of life's details, had now become shattered and torn, unable to stand before the life she once loved.

Before this occurred, I was a happy, confident, and enthusiastic seventeen-year-old; after, almost overnight, I became sad, insecure, and self-conscious. It was as if an earthquake had struck my family and now I was forced to find my way among the rubble without a guide. After the dust began to settle, I no longer recognized my family, my home, or myself.

It was this death that eventually led me to a recovery of faith. Since a vital figure in the foundation of my life had been uprooted, I was driven to seek another one, one that when "the rain fell, and the floods came, and the winds blew and beat upon that house . . . it did not fall, because it had been founded on the rock" (Matthew 7:25).

Encountering the fragility of life at such an intimate level led me to pray in a way I never had before. Instead of just murmuring prayers I'd learned as a child, I began to pray from the very depths of my pain and confusion. Sometimes I yelled at God, asking why he allowed this to happen. Sometimes I cried, begging God for help and strength. Other times I tried bargaining with God, promising to do something for him if he would heal my mother. Despite my persistent efforts to force God to act, her depression only got worse. God appeared, if not deaf, then at the very least, not interested in helping me.

As weeks and months passed, I began to notice a strange phenomenon occurring. I was beginning to experience a mysterious strength inside of me, one that enabled me to stand face-to-face with this suffering, instead of running from it as I usually did. In the midst of this heartache, instead of feeling alone and abandoned by God, I began to feel a Presence accompanying me on this journey, consoling me and embracing my entire being. Instead of continually asking why, I began to consider how I could help my mom and be with her in her suffering. Finally, after a long and dark winter, the first signs of spring were beginning to blossom in me.

I am reminded not only of this event but also of the many "deaths" I have had to undergo in life each season of fall. Despite how difficult some "deaths" were, after each one I experienced a resurrection to something more profound than I could have ever imagined. If someone would have told me years ago that God would use my mother's depression to bring about a deeper conversion in me, I would have considered that person a fool. Now, many years later, I still remain in awe as I ponder the mystery of God's ways.

The beautiful leaves that surround me each autumn in their glory too must die only to be reborn once again with the passing of time. "Unless a grain of wheat falls into the earth and dies, it remains alone; but if it dies, it bears much fruit" (John 12:24).

Perhaps what scares us most about death is that we can't see beyond it. What will life look like if I lose my job? If I can't have the career I want? If I have cancer? If I die? The truth is, we don't know for sure. But as nature and God himself have revealed, there is something much greater beyond what we can see and understand, if only we can trust in its rhythm and allow it to take us beyond ourselves.

29
THE CONTEMPLATIVE MIND

It was an ordinary weekday Mass. There were twenty to thirty people in attendance, most of whom, I'm guessing, were on their lunch break. In the front pew sat a mother with a young boy. As I walked past them on my way to the altar, the boy's face grew mesmerized as he looked at my vestments.

"Wow, Mommy," he said, as I got closer, "check out his clothes!" I laughed to myself and winked at him as I walked by.

The Mass proceeded as usual. After I read the Gospel, I began to give a short homily. "Mommy, who is that man in the painting?" the young boy cried out. Everyone, including myself, smiled and we all shared a brief moment of laughter. The painting the boy was referring to was an image of St. Francis of Assisi praying in a cave, hanging on the wall directly above where he and his mother were sitting. Despite everyone's good sense of humor, the boy's mother appeared mortified.

Immediately after Mass she came running toward me. "Father, I'm so sorry my son interrupted your homily," she said with a panicked look on her face.

I introduced myself and assured her there was nothing to apologize for. I looked at the boy. He was now staring wide-eyed at another painting—in the sacristy—of the Last Supper. I bent down and asked him, "What do you think of that painting?"

"Wow," he said.

Smiling back, I said, "Yes, I agree."

Jesus says in the Gospel, "Unless you turn and become like children, you will never enter the kingdom of heaven" (Matthew 18:3). Children approach life more as a mystery than as a problem that needs to be solved. They are usually curious and receptive to reality in all its wonder. They are keenly aware that there is more beyond what they can perceive. This is why I believe children are the happiest group of people. Unlike adults, they are not stuck in their minds. They live on the level of what I like to call a "contemplative mind."

For most of us adults, reality is only what our thoughts and senses perceive. In the face of tragedy, for example, many people will conclude there is no God. What our minds and senses are faced with appears to contradict this possibility. How could a loving God allow this? we ask. The logic is consistent; however, it is limited by our own minds, or what I like to call our "thinking minds."

St. Paul writes, "We look not to the things that are seen but to the things that are unseen; for the things that are seen are transient, but the things that are unseen are eternal" (2 Corinthians 4:18). What St. Paul is contrasting, I believe, is the difference between these thinking and contemplative minds. The first is limited. The second peers into eternity.

As long as we live in this world, our thinking minds serve a necessary function: they remind us of the extraordinary gap that exists between what our minds can comprehend and what actually exists. After Job has asked God a series of questions from his thinking mind, God responds, "Where were you when I laid the foundation of the earth?" (Job 38:4). This response, though humbling, is not meant to discredit Job's questions, but to remind him that he stands before the Eternal and Infinite One, and not a finite creature like himself created from the dust of the earth.

Shortly after I entered religious life as a still-young man, a wise monk told me, "God is like the air, completely available, yet once we try to grasp at it, it is gone." At the time, I was not able to understand his point because I was convinced I understood God. Many years later, I can honestly say that I still do not understand completely, but thankfully, there are children to remind me that I don't have to.

AN UNUSUAL CHRISTMAS

Your father is recovering well," the doctor assured us. "He should be ready for a visit in a few minutes."

My sister and I breathed a sigh of relief. Although it was a routine heart procedure, our father's declining health left both of us a bit nervous. "Thank God," I whispered, realizing that I was perhaps more nervous than I expected. Then I picked up a magazine from a nearby table as my sister began to notify her friends on Facebook that the procedure went well and thanked everyone for their prayers.

A few minutes later a voice came over the intercom. "Code blue, code blue, all available doctors report to the cardiac care unit immediately." Alarms began to ring, and within seconds a sea of doctors came flooding through the doors that led to the cardiac unit where my father was. My sister and I turned to each other in panic. "Oh no!" we both said. "That's Dad!"

While doctors were speaking with him, Dad's face had turned blue and his heart had stopped. Dad's lungs had filled with fluid, not due to the heart procedure itself, but from the anesthesia and the amount of time he spent lying on his stomach. Thankfully, they were able to resuscitate him and bring him back to life quickly, even as my sister and I watched in horror.

A week later, on Christmas Eve, he finally left the hospital. Despite an exhausting week, we were grateful, not only that our dad was alive, but that he was home and able to celebrate Christmas with us.

As I unpacked his belongings at home, Dad sat in the living room, staring out the window.

"Jeremiah," he said.

"Yes, Dad."

"Are we going to have Mass tonight?"

I froze after hearing his question. *Why tonight?* I thought. When I am at home I usually celebrate Mass in the morning. Suddenly I realized why he was asking. It was Christmas Eve! Amid all the panic and confusion of the past week, I'd lost track of time and forgotten what day it was.

"Oh yeah, of course," I said. "What time?"

"How about 8:00 PM? I need to rest here for a while."

"Okay, that sounds good."

Then a touch of sadness enveloped my heart. One of the gifts of living in a religious community is the shared celebration of certain holy days, Christmas being high on that list. During these celebrations, I am surrounded by people who, though different in age and life experience, both love and care for me in a way that is, for lack of a better word, familial. Along with the fraternal support of brothers and sisters in the faith, the celebration of these holy days includes beautiful music, a reverent liturgy, and an engaging homily that naturally lifts one's mind and heart to higher things. This year, however, my Christmas celebration was going to be very different from what I had become accustomed to.

My father lives alone in a simple two-bedroom trailer. When I was ordained a priest several years ago, we converted his other bedroom into a chapel, so that when I come home I have a place to celebrate Mass and pray. This Christmas Eve, rather than celebrating Mass with my community, this humble spare bedroom that can only fit four to five people comfortably became my church. With me, my dad, my sister, my brother-in-law, and my two nephews in attendance, we were at full capacity.

When my family gathered later that day for Mass, there was no beautiful music sung and no engaging homily given. My father was too tired to utter any of the Mass parts, and my sister and her family tried their best to fill in for the congregation. When it came time for me to read the Gospel, I was deeply moved by these words: "All this took place to fulfil what the Lord had spoken by the prophet: 'Behold, the virgin shall conceive and bear a son, and his name shall be called Emmanuel' (which means, God with us)" (Matthew 1:22–23).

After I read those words, I looked at Dad, standing with the support of a cane, his face still wearing the shock of all he went through. The words "God with us" were ringing in my heart. Suddenly, in this small trailer, without any of the usual bells and whistles, I felt myself being led to a deeper experience of Christmas than I had ever had before.

When we gaze on a Nativity scene, we can often forget the mysterious and confusing background that preceded this divine moment. Nine months earlier, when Mary is visited by the angel Gabriel, she is "greatly troubled" (Luke 1:29) and must be told by the angel, "Do not be afraid, Mary" (Luke 1:30). Despite the dizzying and overwhelming nature of such an encounter, Mary says yes to God, without ever being given a detailed account of how this mystery will unfold. Joseph himself, once he discovers that Mary is pregnant, is understandably confused, and decides to divorce her. In fact, his confusion is so reasonable that an angel must appear to reveal the cause of this event: "Do not fear to take Mary your wife, for that which is conceived in her is of the Holy Spirit" (Matthew 1:20–21).

Joseph and Mary must allow themselves to be led by God. Even though they are both major figures in the drama of salvation history, God only reveals to them what is necessary to make the next step of faith. They cannot see into the future, nor can they trust in things like wealth or status to protect them. Their hope is in God, and their only strength is their faith, which ironically not only will enable shepherds to glorify God but will also enable the Magi, the wise men from the east, to discover the true wisdom they had been seeking their entire life.

As I stood in our little chapel that Christmas Eve and spent a few moments of silence reflecting on the Gospel, I felt a special kinship to Joseph and Mary. Like them, I didn't know where God was leading me, and like them, the birth of Jesus Christ not only gave me hope and consolation in the present moment but also reminded me of a truth so great that something even as cruel as death cannot take away: God is with us.

Many people, including me, are often perplexed before the enormous amount of pain and suffering in our world. "Why doesn't God do something?" we ask. "Why is God silent?" God's answer to our perplexity is much deeper than merely taking away our pain and suffering. God does what is, quite honestly, utterly inconceivable: he becomes one of us. He does this by entering our world, not as a vengeful ruler or an angry judge, but as a defenseless and needy baby. St. John states it in these theological terms: "the Word became flesh" (John 1:14).

As we finished the Mass that night, my sister and I helped Dad get ready for bed. After kissing him goodnight, I felt my heart and my mind finally begin to relax. I felt a deep peace about not knowing exactly what will happen with my father. Rather than entertain all the possible things that could now go wrong with his health, I reminded myself once again that in the birth of Jesus Christ we are given an eternal pledge that God is with us. That's the best Christmas gift we could ever receive and the only one we really need.

31
BECOMING PRESENT

My years as a priest, spiritual director, and confessor have confirmed for me an important fact about humanity: we spend little time in reality. The reason, I believe, is because we are blind and unable to see the utter beauty, depth, and mystery of the present moment. We are, for the most part, futuristic people, spending our lives pursuing, anticipating, and defending ourselves against things to come, most of which never happen.

Throughout the Gospels Jesus reveals his divinity in the most human moments. Martha and Mary are mourning their brother Lazarus when Jesus raises him from the dead (John 11:17–44). He performs his first miracle at the wedding of friends in Cana (John 2:1–10). Jesus calls Levi, a tax collector, in the middle of a workday (Luke 5:27–29).

These Gospel narratives, and many others, show Jesus entering the present moment to be with us. We don't have to manipulate, organize, or control reality for God to be present. He already is. The problem is, we are not.

There is a part of us that wants to put on our "spiritual makeup"—in other words, have our lives together— so that when God visits us we are ready, the way a bride might prepare for the day of her wedding. "I can't be ready for him now," we often say. "I'm too busy with household tasks, I'm still distracted at prayer, or there is too much going on at the office right now." Once we get control of these situations, we think, then we will be ready for God. The problem is, despite our resistance, and our failure to see the sacredness of the present moment, the Bridegroom is waiting: "Behold, I stand at the door and knock" (Revelation 3:20).

People often ask me, "How can I grow in the spiritual life?" I think what they are really asking is, *How can I experience more deeply the presence of God in my life?* My answer is always, "Learn to live in the present moment." The reason I say this, of course, is because the present moment is where we find God.

In the face of such apparent simplicity, we are often confronted with two conflicting experiences. Our hearts are relieved to hear that God is already present in our life, not in an abstract or philosophical way, but in the bare simplicity of the present moment. Our minds, however, can be annoyed by such a seemingly elementary approach to spirituality. But they don't have to be.

A few months ago, I made a radical decision in my life: I was going to try to do only one thing at a time. If I was cooking, I was just going to cook. If I was praying, I was just going to pray. If I was driving, I was just going to drive. What else could you do, one might ask, while you are cooking, driving, or praying? A million other things. How easy it is to talk on the phone, text a friend, listen to music, organize the next month, recall some memory, arrange our thoughts for our next conservation, when we are engaged in the ordinary activities of daily life.

Since I began this experiment, God has taught me that I don't need more time, talent, or technology to live a meaningful life. I already have it. Whether it is the traffic jam I am in, the people I live with, or the people I am preaching to, each one of these moments reveals God's love for me. When I can learn to pay attention to life as it really is and reject the temptation to escape reality through various daydreams and fantasies, I experience, in a subtle and mysterious way, the presence of God in each moment.

Multitasking, despite popular opinion, is not a gift. Occasionally it is necessary, but as a way of life it reinforces our deep-seated fear that our lives are incomplete and that we are alone. Contrary to this attitude, Jesus tells us, "Do not be anxious about your life. . . . If God so clothes the grass of the field, which today is alive and tomorrow is thrown into the oven, will he not much more clothe you, O men of little faith" (Matthew 6:25, 30).

The present moment, I am learning, is the only place where this abandonment can occur. It is neither a prison cell nor a tropical island. It is enough, and it is exactly what we need.

LISTENING

The only way I can have a conversation with my nephews, ages twelve and eighteen, is if I take away their phones. Even when I do, eye contact is kept to a minimum and their bodies appear unable to relax without a piece of technology in their hand. This is becoming true for many adults as well. It seems that we spend more time listening to devices than to one another.

When I was in school studying spiritual direction, my teachers continually emphasized that spiritual direction is a ministry of listening. After the lectures each morning, we were given the opportunity to practice our listening. Each student was paired up with another student. One was given the role of the director, and the other was the directee. The directee was asked to share the contents of their prayer from the previous twenty-four hours, while the director was told merely to listen. The only time the director was allowed to talk was when he would summarize, in a concise manner, the content of what the directee was sharing. The reason for this was simply to make sure the director really heard, was listening, to what the directee was saying.

As I listened to all my directees, who varied in age, occupation, and vocation, I immediately realized a problem. I was only half listening, while my other half was problem solving. I wanted to give my directees advice, quote something from a saint, or impress them with my knowledge of the Bible and spirituality. If it was a younger person, I wanted to tell them my experience and what happened to me when I was their age. If someone began to cry, I wanted to console them and tell them it was going to be all right. What I really wanted, I realize now, was for them to stop telling their story and for me to start telling mine.

Listening to another person, I learned, means to receive the other person as they are, in their joy and sorrow, happiness and pain, with their strengths and weaknesses, without turning their life into a problem that needs to be solved by me. It means, essentially, to accept the mystery of the other person, and to allow that person to remain a mystery, without reducing them to our human categories, labels, and stereotypes, which, unfortunately, we often resort to.

A few years ago, I made an eight-day directed retreat with a priest who had a reputation for being a gifted spiritual director. After we met on the first evening, we had decided that I would pray four hours a day and meet with him each evening to discuss the contents of my prayer. On the second evening I met him in his room and he asked, "How was your prayer today?" I started sharing with him how my prayer was going, and I would pause at times because I thought he would want to interject a correction, offer some words of wisdom, or give me some advice. He was completely silent. At the end our time he said, "Okay, see you tomorrow."

Even though he didn't say anything, I knew that I was sincerely listened to. I did not feel judged, labeled, or analyzed. I did feel, however, accepted, in a way I may never have before. As my retreat continued, our meetings followed the same format. "How was your prayer today?" he would ask, and then I would start talking. Since I wasn't expecting him to interrupt me anymore, I was given the freedom to explore all that God was doing inside my soul. Without projecting his own experience of God or life on me, I was enabled the freedom to discover my own. A whole new world was unearthed inside of me, and through this spiritual director's listening presence, the mystery of God's ways and his healing became a tangible reality that I continue to marvel at many years later.

I have come to believe not only that spiritual direction is a ministry of listening but also that life is a ministry of listening. Whether it is prayer, marriage, or friendship, listening to another person—God, a spouse, or a friend—becomes an opportunity for grace. Of course there are moments in life when listening may not be enough. A correction, a disagreement, or perhaps a command needs to happen. What I have learned, surprisingly, is that even when those difficult moments come along, if I have genuinely listened to the other person, the reception of that correction or command is at least considered more thoughtfully.

The person who is being listened to acquires the freedom and the space to struggle without immediately feeling judged or analyzed. The listener has the opportunity to participate in God's patient and unconditional love. The challenge for both of them is learning how to do this in a world filled with noise and distraction. The guide for both of them is the One who always listens to us.

33
POST-RETREAT DEPRESSION

The last day of every retreat is the same. I wake up, usually after not sleeping well, feeling a bit sad and annoyed.

I am sad because, however long the retreat lasted, it had been a time of quiet joy with God and the few people I was called to lead on this retreat. The retreat center, even if located in the middle of the city, became an oasis from the noise and busyness of modern living, allowing each person the space to decompress, unwind, and perhaps for the first time in a while, be alone with God. I am annoyed because the retreat is over. This idyllic situation, unlike any other in this world, is disappearing before my eyes, and there is nothing I can do about it. I hear retreatants packing their bags, making travel plans, and beginning to say goodbye to one another. Trying to appear stoic, I smile, thank everyone for coming, and say goodbye to each person, while interiorly my heart feels barren and alone. I have what I like to call, PRD, post-retreat depression.

During each retreat, I tell everyone that this is a special time of grace. God often "lifts the veil" and allows us to encounter him in a way that is different from our ordinary daily life experience. No matter how blessed a time the retreat was, most of us are not called to live on the mountain alone with God. We have families, jobs, and communities that, whether we like it or not, are waiting for us. The key, I emphasize, is to integrate our experience on retreat into our daily lives.

One area of difficulty for people who had a profound experience of God on retreat is the almost complete identification of an experience of God with God. As a retreat director, I have witnessed countless people have life-changing experiences in the course of a retreat, especially retreats that include a heavy dose of silence and solitude. After these experiences, the typical response is, "I don't want to leave here." This is, perhaps to our surprise, a natural human response. Anytime we experience anything that brings joy, comfort, or pleasure, we don't want to let go of it. In fact, we often grasp at it and try desperately to force it to stay.

This is demonstrated almost verbatim in the Gospel account of the Transfiguration. Jesus has taken Peter, James, and John up a mountain, a symbol of going on retreat and preparing the way for a deeper encounter with God. There, in silence and solitude, Jesus is transfigured before them: "His face shone like the sun, and his garments became white as light" (Matthew 17:2). In the midst of this profound encounter with the Lord, Peter proclaims, "Lord, it is well that we are here; if you wish, I will make three booths here, one for you and one for Moses and one for Elijah" (Matthew 17:4).

Peter, in his all-too-human attempt to hold on to this precious moment, is basically asking, "Do we really have to leave?" The experience of the transfigured Lord, like our own deeper experiences of the Lord on retreat, is one he is not ready yet to let go of. A few verses later, however, Jesus and the three chosen disciples are already coming down the mountain. Their retreat has abruptly finished, and now they are returning to daily life.

What is the point of the Transfiguration for the three disciples who witnessed it? Shortly afterward, Jesus's passion begins. In a matter of moments, Jesus will move from being the transfigured Lord to the Lord who is betrayed, beaten, and crucified. The Passion, at least exteriorly, will appear as a contradiction of Jesus's own words that he is "the light of the world" and the one "who follows me will not walk in darkness" (John 8:12). Ultimately, the Transfiguration is meant to strengthen the faith of the disciples so that in the midst of the confusion and darkness of the Passion that's to come, their faith remains steadfast.

A similar reasoning, I believe, can be used to understand why God gives us consoling and beautiful experiences of him, whether it is on retreat, during prayer, or just simply in the middle of our daily lives. They are meant to strengthen us. In many ways, they are a quiet reminder from God that our lives, despite what we may feel and experience, are governed by God's fatherly care. What is perhaps most frustrating about these experiences is that we cannot, despite our best efforts, control or create them. There is no method of prayer, retreat director, or special place that can cause them to occur more frequently or in the manner we desire. They are completely God's gift to us, given when and how he sees fit. They are meant to be received with joy and gratitude.

Even though I remind retreatants of this at the end of every retreat, I still find myself slipping into PRD. Despite the duration of the retreat, I witnessed firsthand God's love breaking more deeply into a person's life. That person, despite their own fears and struggles and sometimes even because of them, becomes an icon of God's relentless pursuit, not only of their soul, but of mine as well. Like Peter, I have often asked God in the silence of my own heart, "Do we really have to leave?"

Shortly after each retreat ends, I'm separated from those with whom I spent a few days alone on the mountain with Jesus. The intimacy, silence, and peace that we shared together are now behind us. Now, against my own will, I wait at an airport filled with strangers, noise, and activity. Occasionally, on the flight home the person I am seated beside will initiate some kind of spiritual conversation (my clothing, is a giveaway that I might be interested!), but generally the flight is a quiet one. I spend the majority of the time reflecting on the past few days and praying for those with whom I shared this journey.

There is a temptation to believe that after every retreat I am now plunged back down to the base of the mountain and must wait again for the next retreat to begin my ascent. With this mindset, life appears as an obstacle to our continuing growth in holiness. The reality is, because of this retreat, or a deeper experience of God in general, I am not plunged back down at the bottom once it is over, but I am actually at a higher elevation because of my experience.

One day, God willing, we will reach the peak of that mountain. And so we continue our ascent, confident that God is guiding us to the peak of that mountain where he has already prepared a place for us.

34
WAKING UP

I was suddenly shaken out of my daydream by the sound of sirens ringing in the distance. As I looked in my rearview mirror, a police car was quickly approaching behind me. Any moment now, I thought, the police car would pass me and catch the culprit they were in pursuit of. Instead, I was surprised when, as the police car got closer to me, it did not change lanes to pass. The culprit the police were in pursuit of was me!

I pulled over to the shoulder not knowing exactly what was going on. Was I speeding? I didn't think so. Did I run a red light? Not that I remember. Feeling confused and somewhat afraid, I rolled down my window to greet the officer who was approaching my car.

"Good morning," I said.

"Good morning," the officer echoed back, without a smile or a hint of sincerity. "Do you know what the speed limit is, sir?"

"Sixty-five?" I said, somewhat unsure.

"It's fifty-five," she said. "Do you know how fast you were driving?"

"Sixty?" I said.

"I clocked you at seventy-seven."

"Seventy-seven!" I said in astonishment. "Are you sure?"

"These machines don't lie, sir. I'll be right back," she said.

As she went back to her police car, I sat there confused and a bit alarmed that I was driving so fast without even being aware of it. After a few minutes, I was beginning to wonder what was taking her so long. This was the first time I had been pulled over and therefore could not fathom what she was doing. I looked in my mirror and saw her writing and on the phone. Finally, she got out and approached my car.

"You were driving twenty-two miles over the speed limit, sir. Here is your ticket. Your fine will be $300 and you will receive six points on your driving record. Please slow down," she said, all without a smile.

As I returned to the friary later that day, my body was tense and my heart was troubled. What bothered me most was not getting a speeding ticket, but that I was completely unaware that I was engaging in something so potentially dangerous, not only for me, but for others as well. This police officer, in a strange and rather expensive way, was a messenger from God, reminding me to wake up and start paying attention, before I or somebody else gets hurt due to my lack of attention.

The New Testament is filled with similar admonitions. "Stay awake," Jesus warns us, "for you do not know on what day your Lord is coming" (Matthew 24:42 NAB). St. Paul warns the Thessalonians, "So then let us not sleep, as others do, but let us keep awake" (1 Thessalonians 5:6), while Jesus utters these sobering words in the book of Revelation: "Behold, I am coming like a thief! Blessed is he who is awake" (Revelation 16:15).

What exactly is the New Testament exhorting us to wake up from? Essentially it is any life, or any part of our life, that does not have God at its center. Those of us who consider ourselves fairly devout can easily assume that this does not apply to us. *After all*, we might conclude, *I pray every day, I'm involved in ministry, and I am living a moral life. I am awake!* Without even realizing it, certain aspects of our Christian life can be operating more on our own strength, intelligence, and creativity than actual dependence on God.

We should all honestly ask ourselves the important question, Is God really at the center of our lives? Unfortunately, one of the only ways we can discern this is through trials. What are we like when prayer is dry? Do we give up because God doesn't seem to be entertaining us and filling us with consolation? What is our response to sickness or some form of bodily weakness? Do we get mad at God for interrupting the hopes and plans we made for our life? What is our attitude toward ministry when, on a human level, it appears to be failing? Do we lose heart and consider giving up because something is not working the way we imagined?

Occasionally, people are taken aback when I say that God can use something like sickness, divorce, or bankruptcy as part of our ongoing conversion. Of course, God does not will that we experience any of these; rather, he uses them to bring about a greater good, which is essentially our own deeper conversion and growth in holiness. They are often a wakeup call for us: for those who are distracted and driving at a dangerous speed, and even for those who aren't, they help us to continue moving ahead with greater clarity and resolve.

Like the Good Shepherd, he seeks us out when we go astray, and like a loving Father, he draws us closer even when we remain at his side. Whether these moments produce joy or suffering, God is teaching us that our faith and our trust can only be in him. He will use whatever it takes to get us back on track, refocus, and reach our destination, where he is already waiting for us.

A PATH OF INTIMACY

Every month I meet individually with many people to discuss their relationship with God. This includes men and women of different ages, vocations, and life experiences. Each one has sought spiritual direction because they want greater intimacy with God. Despite this common desire, each person's relationship with God is as unique as the individual. In the spiritual life, after all, there are no identical twins.

Each individual meeting lasts about an hour. Depending on what each person is sharing on a particular day, sometimes there are tears, sometimes there is laughter, and sometimes there are both within the same meeting. These responses are not because of emotional or psychological problems, but because these are people of prayer. In their prayer they are encountering the living God who, although he desires to be known, never allows us to grasp him completely. This seemingly intimate and yet distant aspect of God can cause joy and happiness one day, fear and anxiety the next.

I am by no means an expert in the ways of God. A spiritual director is not a guru who has all the answers, nor an expert in discerning exactly what God is doing in your life. I'm also not, as most spiritual directors are not, a psychologist who is looking to discover the causes behind one's behavior, emotional outlook, or mental state.

A spiritual director is not even necessarily what we'd call a friend. Although friendly in nature, the monthly meetings between a spiritual director and a directee are not the equivalent of two friends getting coffee and catching up on each other's life. Since God is the center of this relationship, the space that a director and directee occupy is surrounded in mystery, which is why this relationship defies worldly categories.

A spiritual director is simply someone who assists another in his relationship with God. They do this most effectively when they listen, without an agenda, to a person's experience of God, particularly in an individual's prayer life. This listening helps the other person hear God's communication in their own life and notice how they are responding.

People often ask me if they need a spiritual director. My answer is always the same: if you desire to take the gospel seriously, then I highly recommend one. The reason for this is simple: each of us needs help. By ourselves, we are unable to perceive God's action in our lives. The Christian life flourishes, not when we live in isolation from others, but when we can share the joys and struggles with another believer, who not only desires to see our relationship with God grow, but who is mature enough to sit with us and listen to us as we sift through a wide range of emotions and experiences.

It wasn't until I entered religious life that I began receiving spiritual direction on a regular basis. As a novice, I was assigned a spiritual director with whom I was required to meet each month whether I felt like it or not. It was during those monthly meetings that I discovered a startling realization: God desires me. I came to this realization, not so much through what my director said, but simply through the process of direction itself.

Speaking to another person about my relationship with God on a regular basis enabled me to notice God's action in my life more deeply. My desire for prayer, my love for the poor, and the joy I experienced in my religious vocation became clear signs of God's grace in my life that, were it not for spiritual direction, would have most likely gone unnoticed.

Of course, these graces are not reserved for consecrated religious only. They are available for everyone and should be a part, in various degrees, in every Christian's life. Yet the question remains: How do I find a spiritual director? Most people believe, unfortunately, that only a priest can be a spiritual director, but actually most priests are not spiritual directors. Priesthood and spiritual direction are two separate ministries, rarely found together in an individual. A good spiritual director has three essential qualities. First, God has called them to this ministry. Second, they are a person of deep prayer who is striving to conform his life to the gospel. Finally, they must be a good listener. If a person possesses these three qualities, whether that person is a priest, religious, layman, or laywoman, is irrelevant.

Regardless of whether we can find an official spiritual director in our life, each of us needs somebody with whom we can share the joys and struggles that occur in our relationship with God. This other person becomes, perhaps without even realizing it, a mirror that enables us to see things we were previously unaware of. Without such a person we run the risk of remaining trapped inside our own narrow and limited perspectives and can fail to recognize the grace of God that is being given to us now. As my current spiritual director has often said, "Only a fool directs himself."

36
FORTY DAYS (AFTER)

After forty days of solitude and silence, I was convinced I would leave my hermitage a new man. What exactly I would look like I wasn't sure, but at the very least I imagined myself a stronger, wiser, and more loving person. I pictured myself returning home to my community, eager to serve the other brothers, willing to listen to everyone who sought my attention, and no longer getting frustrated and annoyed when things did not go my way. After all, I had just done something I once thought was impossible: I spent forty days alone in a hermitage in the middle of the woods.

On a surface level, my days in hermitage were dreadfully boring. There were no news flashes, text messages, or phone calls. Whether I was eating, praying, or walking, I tried to surrender each moment to God by simply saying, "Here I am" (Genesis 22:1; Exodus, 3:4; 1 Samuel 3:4). Whatever occurred next, whether it was a group of deer running through the woods, a fresh snowfall, or a sensible experience of God's presence, I was learning a key lesson that solitude teaches: God is always near, but we are far away.

Providentially, my retreat coincided with Holy Week and Easter, leaving me an ample amount of nourishment in the liturgy and the Scriptures. After the beautiful yet somber liturgies of Holy Thursday and Good Friday, I spent almost all of Holy Saturday sitting by a lake, allowing these mysteries to sink more deeply into my heart and mind. As I was preparing to celebrate the Easter Vigil that night, I wanted to send a text message to the entire world reminding them that "God so loved the world that he gave his only Son" (John 3:16), or run through the nearest town screaming, "This is how much God loves you." Fortunately, I didn't do either, but another important lesson was given to me: life with God is never boring.

Perhaps my most cherished moments of retreat were the hours I was able to spend in silent prayer. Each day I would spend, on average, three hours in this contemplative posture before God, not speaking to him in words or even using my mind to reflect on him, but just resting in his presence. Occasionally, when I experienced a brief pause from the thinking, analyzing, and worrying that my mind is usually occupied with, there was a profound stillness waiting for me on the other side.

This stillness of course was not just the result of a quieted mind, but an encounter with a Presence whose warmth and gentleness no words or thoughts could contain. If I was ever experiencing any loneliness or fear, these precious hours of prayer had a mysterious way of reminding me that I was not crazy for wanting to make this retreat, as some believed, but that God had led me here. Then another important lesson was given to me: prayer reveals to us, not our desire for God, but God's desire for us.

But despite all this abundant grace poured on me during this time of retreat, I am still me. I remain selfish, stubborn, and lazy. Although I have experienced God's love on such an intimate level, I am still tempted to look elsewhere for consolation, whether through worldly means, human praise, or even spiritual applause. While spending hours in silence and prayer brought deep peace and joy to my soul, it did not remove the wounds, hurts, and pains that have accumulated in my heart during the course of my life. Solitude did not eliminate my humanity and my need for redemption. Oddly enough, it only affirmed its necessity.

Unconsciously, I had hoped this retreat would get rid of all this human stuff, so that I could move on to more "spiritual" things. So I was caught off guard when, after the retreat was over, I felt not saintly or angelic but utterly human.

As I was driving home a part of me was tempted to view it all as a disappointment, since this retreat had appeared to produce no immediate changes within me. I had forgotten, rather quickly, another spiritual lesson: God's grace at work in a soul is often imperceptible to our human senses. Therefore, we must always be slow in judging and evaluating God's work in others and ourselves.

It would be wrong to claim that after forty days of solitude and silence nothing has changed. Transformation has occurred, just not the way I expected it. I have noticed, since I left the hermitage, that my heart has become more open, less afraid, and more willing to engage the uncomfortable moments of life I once used to flee from. I am able, thanks to the deepening encounter with God's love I experienced in solitude, to accept more readily the poverty of my own humanity, which, in turn, helps me to accept more easily the poverty of others. Finally, I am becoming more aware of God's presence, not only in the more "spiritual" moments of my life, but in the ordinary, mundane, and trivial moments of life in which we all find ourselves.

If someone would have told me forty days ago that this would be the fruit of my time in hermitage, most likely I would have been unimpressed. These fruits, I thought, appear so minor compared to the change I believed I needed.

As I was walking to my car, I did not feel like a spiritual giant, but more like a spiritual beginner. Instead of feeling holy and spiritually rejuvenated, I felt weak and vulnerable. But this weakness and vulnerability didn't leave me sad or afraid. This realization contained a degree of purity and freshness, the way a home appears after it has been thoroughly cleaned. Perhaps during these forty days of retreat, God's desire was not necessarily to build a new house, but merely to clean the one he had already built.

37
BRINGING IT TO COMPLETION

Several weeks ago, I received some of the happiest news of my life: a publishing company contacted me and informed me of their interest in publishing a series of reflections I sent them three months earlier. I was so shocked that I said, somewhat embarrassingly, to the editor on the phone, "Are you serious . . . really publish it . . . as a book?"

Laughing, he said, "Yes, I am serious, a real book. We really like what you sent us."

He began to speak about some of the details of publishing, mentioning words like contracts, royalties, and deadlines. As soon as he began speaking, I was swept away by a euphoric feeling of joy and gratitude. "Maybe I wasn't wasting my time, all these years, with my writing," I said to myself. "I can't believe this is happening. Thank you, Lord."

"There is only one problem," he said.

Immediately, my daydream came to a screeching halt.

"Your manuscript is currently at twenty thousand words. We need it to be closer to twice that before we have a real book. So, keep writing. We will set a deadline for six months."

There was a long pause.

"Father," he said, "are you there?"

"Yes," I said, hesitantly and feeling like I had just been punched in the stomach, "I am here."

"Good. Now, our contracts people will email you the contract in a few days. Please read through it and sign it so we can begin the process. In the meantime, keep writing. I look forward to seeing how this project progresses."

"Um, thank you. Me too."

I hung up the phone and began to experience a dramatic shift in my emotions. My joy and gratitude quickly turned into anxiety and fear.

"How am I going to write twenty thousand words in six months?" I said to myself. "I am a priest with other responsibilities. I have homilies and retreats to prepare, spiritual direction appointments to attend to, responsibilities from my own religious community to fulfill. I am not a full-time writer. I can't do this. Why did I ever start writing this book in the first place? I should have known that I don't have time for this."

❇ ❇ ❇

Whenever I'm given a task, regardless of its nature, there is a subtle voice that whispers inside me, "You can't do this."

This voice has followed me for as long as I can remember. After my "reversion" to Catholicism at age eighteen, a voice kept whispering, "You are going to lose all of your friends. Everybody is going to laugh at you when they see you praying and going to church. You will never be able to withstand it. You care too much what people think."

When I was discerning joining the Franciscans, a voice kept telling me, "You can't live in New York City. You're from the country. It will be too much for you."

A few years ago, when I began to spend extended periods of time in hermitage, a voice kept saying, "Who do you think you are spending all this time in solitude? Look how weak and insecure you are; you will go crazy. You can't do it."

St. Ignatius of Loyola believes that each person must contend with three voices in their lives: the voice of God, the voice of the devil, and the voice of one's own humanity. Each voice, like each person, has a distinctive character to it. The voice of God, generally, is uplifting, encouraging, and loving, lifting one's heart and mind to higher things, while the voice of the devil is filled with discouragement, negativity, and sadness, leaving a soul entirely earthbound in its pursuits, pleasures, and vision. The voice of one's own humanity is not always so clear. Perhaps it can be a mixture of both, depending on one's own history and life decisions. Regardless of which voice is speaking, St. Paul's reminder to the Ephesians is an appropriate one: "For we are not contending against flesh and blood" (Ephesians 6:12). Reality contains many other powers or forces that are always present, even if we don't often perceive them.

For these reasons, after the conversation with my new editor at the publishing house, the real question for me was not, How will I finish this book? but, Which voices will I listen to? I will finish this book the way I have accomplished everything in my life: with God's grace. If God wills something for us, his grace is never lacking. Every time the voice of discouragement has appeared in my life, it has always proved to be false. I returned to the Church despite what my friends thought. I spent many wonderful years living in New York City as a Franciscan. And despite my weaknesses and insecurity I have spent a significant amount of time in hermitage alone with God, and remain (at least somewhat!) mentally stable.

What God asks of us at times can seem impossible. How can I forgive that person who hurt me? How can I face life with this disease, embarrassment, or failure that is always before me? Instead of feeling strong and confident before God's will, we often feel inadequate and incompetent. Abraham asks God, "Shall a child be born to a man who is a hundred years old?" (Genesis 17:17). The prophet Amos, hoping to escape his vocation, laments, "I was no prophet, nor have I belonged to a company of prophets; I was a shepherd and a dresser of sycamores" (Amos 7:14 NAB). Zechariah asks the angel Gabriel, "How shall I know this? For I am an old man, and my wife is advanced in years" (Luke 1:18). In all these examples, these instances are not the last chapter.

The voice that has been telling me, "You can't do this," cannot be the voice of God. Whether it is the voice of the devil, or my own humanity, or a mixture of both, I must refuse to listen and persevere, while relying completely on God's grace for inspiration and strength.

This is true for each of us. Wherever God's will has us at this moment, we move forward not by asking why or how, but by sifting through the voices until we arrive at the voice of our Father, who loves us, encourages us, and strengthens us for the journey ahead. "I am confident of this, that the one who began a good work in you will continue to complete it, until the day of Christ Jesus" (Philippians 1:6 NAB).

Acknowledgments

I wish to thank the following people for their prayers, support, and friendship: my father, John K. Shryock; my sister, Tammy Turner, and her husband, Chris Turner; Mason and Bradon Turner; the Franciscan Friars and Sisters of the Renewal; the Sisters of Life; Fr. Brian Graebe, STD, without whose editorial skills and support I could never have completed this work; Bonnie E. Grubb; Seth and Molly Taylor; Greg and Roberta Ward; Sefanit Stefanos; Megan Jackson; Yong Oh; Brendan Laracy; Deacon Donald J. Prendergast; Kimberlee Peifer; Cynthia Kin Ryu Taberner; Carmelite Sisters of the Most Sacred Heart of Los Angeles; Michelle Jenkins; Sycamore Tree Retreat Center in Condon, Montana; Cindy Codi; the Monastery of Bethlehem in Livingston Manor, New York; Beth Ferraro; Blake and Christina Robinson; John and Julie Heinen; Kathleen Jones; Dr. Lisa Petronis; Karen Schulze; Jay and Liz Stewart; Dan and Lana Maggio; Briana Maggio; Kristina Maggio; and Msgr. Edward J. Coyle.

About the Author

Fr. Jeremiah Myriam Shryock, CFR, grew up in Barto, Pennsylvania. He graduated from Kutztown University in 2002 with a degree in philosophy. Later that year he entered the Community of Franciscan Friars of the Renewal. In 2011, Timothy Cardinal Dolan ordained him a priest at St. Patrick's Cathedral in New York City. In 2014, Fr. Jeremiah completed studies in spiritual direction at Our Lady of Divine Providence Spiritual Direction School in Clearwater, Florida. As a Franciscan, he has lived in Texas, New Mexico, New York, and New Jersey, where he has served in various levels of formation in his community, ministered to the poor and homeless, and shared in the CFR mission of evangelization. He has recorded over fifty podcasts on various aspects of faith and spirituality (available on "Soundcloud"), and currently lives in his community's House of Prayer in Monticello, New York, where his primary ministry is prayer, spiritual direction, preaching, and retreat work.

San Damiano Books
PARACLETE PRESS

*Wisdom, inspiration, and practical spirituality from the Franciscan
tradition, for people of all denominations, faiths, and backgrounds*

**Francis of Assisi
In His Own Words**

The Essential Writings

*Translated and Annotated
by Jon M. Sweeney*

ISBN 978-1-64060-019-5 | $16.99, Trade paperback

**Francis of Assisi's
Sermon on the Mount**

Lessons from the Admonitions

John Michael Talbot

ISBN 978-1-64060-172-7 | $19.99, Trade paperback

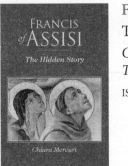

**Francis of Assisi
The Hidden Story**

*Chiara Mercuri,
Translated by Robert Edmonson,* CJ

ISBN 978-1-64060-175-5 | $23, Trade paperback

These and many other titles on Franciscan spirituality
available at bookstores
Paraclete Press | 1-800-451-5006
www.paracletepress.com